W9-CHN-184

DANCE: RITUALS OF EXPERIENCE

Third Edition

The point to be noted here
is not that art of this
traditional Western type
and theoretical knowledge of this
Western kind are not the
most excellent of art
and knowledge of their kind,
but merely that they are but one
type of art and but one type
of knowledge.
There is also the equally
important aesthetic component
in the nature of things
which is genuine knowledge
in its own right.

F.S.C. NORTHROP
The Meeting of East and West

Pearl Primus in *Speak to Me of Rivers,* 1944.

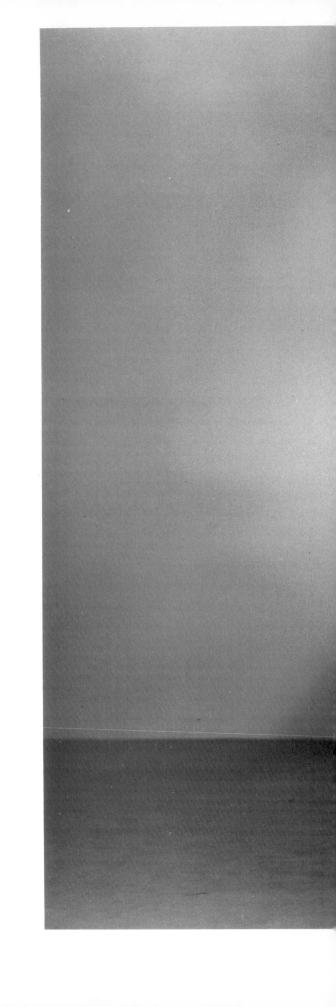

Barbara Morgan

Johan Elbers

Jamake Highwater

Third Edition

DANCE

RITUALS OF EXPERIENCE

Oxford University Press
New York Oxford

FRONT COVER: Edward Villella in *Watermill*.
Photograph by Martha Swope.

FRONTISPIECE: Clive Thompson of The Alvin Ailey Dance Company in John Butler's *Carmina Burana*.

Oxford University Press

Oxford New York
Athens Auckland Bangkok Bombay
Calcutta Cape Town Dar es Salaam Delhi
Florence Hong Kong Istanbul Karachi
Kuala Lumpur Madras Madrid Melbourne
Mexico City Nairobi Paris Singapore
Taipei Tokyo Toronto

and associated companies in
Berlin Ibadan

First published in 1978 by Methuen Publication, Toronto, Canada.

First issued as an Oxford University Press paperback, 1996

Library of Congress Cataloging-in-Publication Data
Highwater, Jamake.
Dance : rituals of experience / Jamake Highwater.—3rd. ed.
p. cm.
Originally published: Pennington, NJ : Princeton Book Co., c1992.
Includes bibliographical references (p.) and index.
ISBN 0-19-511205-9 (Pbk.)
1. Dance—History. 2. Religious dance, Modern—History.
I. Title.
GV1601.H54 1996
792.8—dc20 96-23815

10 9 8 7 6 5 4 3 2 1

Printed in the United States of America

CONTENTS

Ruth Walz, courtesy BAM

Using the past to discover the future; *The Games* by Meredith Monk and Ping Chong (1984); an opus from two of the most important performing artists of the decade.

PREFACE

I don't recall exactly where or when my intrigue with dancing began. But I strongly suspect that as a child I discovered dancing not in films or on the stage but within my own body, for movement has always been an intrinsic power in my life. I probably danced before I began to speak. And when a love of language eventually overtook me, I was endlessly tossed between my desire to write and my desire to dance.

Though the origins of my lifelong fascination with dancing are only dimly remembered, I know for certain that the first choreographers I met and admired were Ruth St. Denis and Lester Horton. Their imprint on my childhood sensibility and my later choreographic style was immense, despite the fact that I was determined to devote myself to writing instead of dancing. Regardless of my intentions, I was persistently drawn to Miss Ruth's studio on Ventura Boulevard and to the storefront theater run by Lester Horton on Melrose Avenue in Los Angeles. Though I thought I wanted to be a writer, my body wanted to be a dancer.

Finally, in San Francisco in the 1960s, I put all but my critical writing aside, and I devoted myself to the presentation of a great variety of companies and soloists and to the creation of my own works for the theater. Producing and presenting various performances gave me an uncommon access to the world of performers and choreographers: Ann Halprin, Erick Hawkins, Jean Erdman, José Limón, the National Dancers of Ceylon, the Bolshoi Ballet, and many other international groups. We talked and we watched each other perform, and all of us grew from the experience. Clearly, those years during which I lived in the dance world have had a vast impact upon my artistic values and my thinking. Yet it was inevitable that I would leave dancing behind and return to my love of literature. It was equally inevitable that I would eventually try to write a book about my experiences among dancers — a book that has had a very special significance to me among my published works because it represents the marriage of literature and dance, the two art forms which have dominated my life.

Milton Oleaga

In memory of

ALAN ALBERT

Nobody knows the trouble I've seen . . .

Scott Douglas and Erin Martin in Glen Tetley's *Sargasso.*

Milton Oleaga

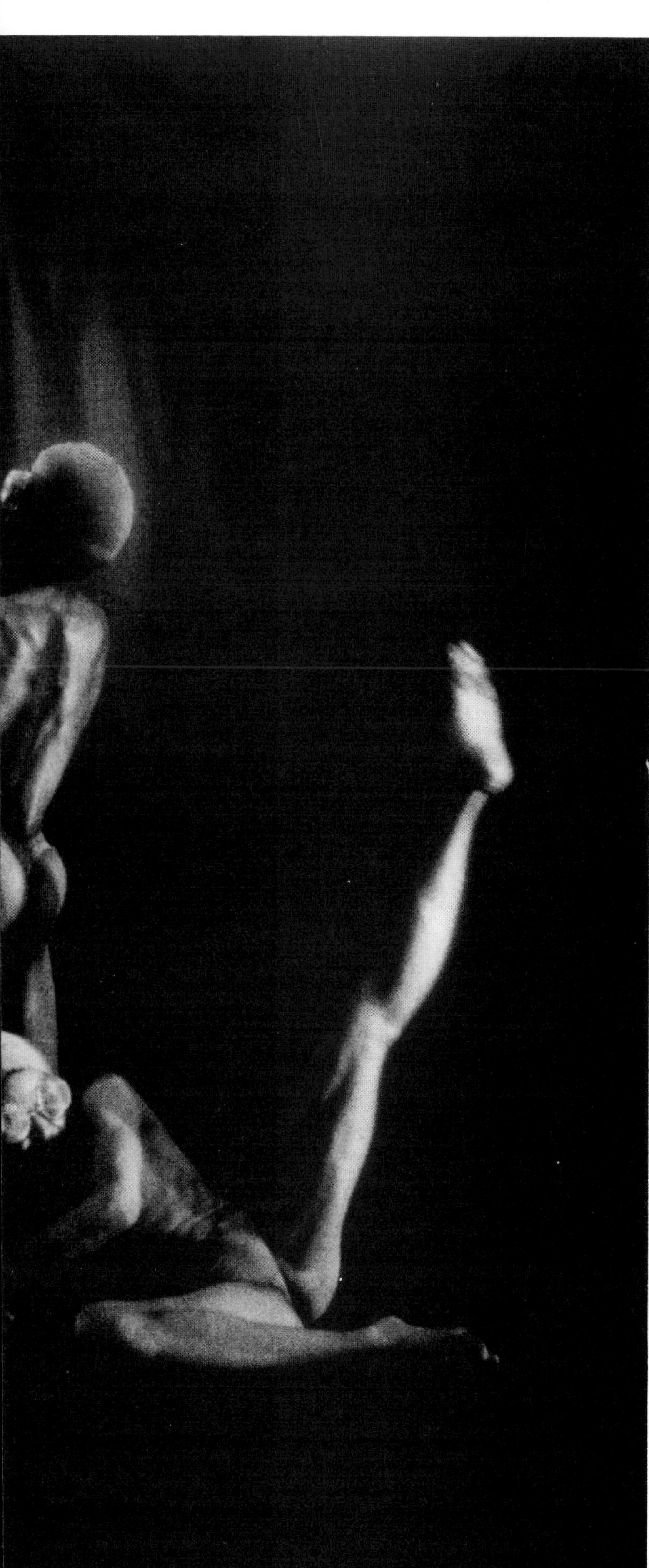

Myths are things
which never happened
but always are.

— SALLUST

Tribal mentality in Afro-American dance is seen in *Prey* by the Fred Benjamin Dance Company.

THE RIPPLE of brown muscles and the holocaust of feeling coming from the stage evoke memories of the Afro-American experience — an art compounded of the mix of cultures and races. But this ritual performance was never intended for a ceremonial ground in an African jungle. It is not part of the complex tribal memory of a people or the result of a shaman's instruction. Rather, the dance was formulated in every detail by choreographer George Faison and relentlessly rehearsed by members of the Alvin Ailey American Dance Theater for presentation to a predominantly white audience at a Broadway theater. For many spectators, the dancing is the quintessence of primitive mysteries, while for others it amounts to Uncle Tom in tights.

The dance is called *Gazelle,* and like many of the Ailey Company works, it is *about* African ritual — though it is not really African and is not actually ritualistic in the formal meaning of the word. But, in an important new sense, *Gazelle* is nonetheless an authentic ritualization of the search of Black Americans for roots. It is a private ritual created by a modern incarnation of the shaman whom we call "the artist."

Whether ritual is tribal or private, it serves an urgent function both for the Blacks who lived for centuries in Africa and produced a rich civilization and for American Blacks who were deprived of their culture when they were abducted. Ritual sustains the life of a people by reshaping "nationalistic" experience into a significant form unique to the culture which produces it. Ritual is not a product of *primitive* people. Rather, it is produced by all peoples still in touch with the capacity to express themselves in metaphor. Though ritual is primal, it is not primitive. It is neither simple, crude, nor barbaric. To the contrary, ritual is a complex, pervasive, and remarkably human process which exists everywhere in history and everywhere on Earth. It gives people an access to the ineffable and it provides them with ways of dealing with forces which seem beyond their comprehension and control.

There are two kinds of ritual. The first, studied by ethnologists, is familiar to us: it is an unself-conscious act without deliberate "aesthetic" concerns, arriving from anonymous tribal influences over many generations and epitomizing the group's fundamental value system. The second form of ritual is new: it is the creation of an exceptional individual who transforms his or her experience into a metaphoric idiom known as "art." These two ritual forms necessarily overlap. There is no question that idiosyncratic art is highly influenced by tribal rites. This process is visible in the works of many twentieth-century artists of a highly individual style: Maurice de Vlaminck and André Derain altered the development of art when they discovered African masks and conveyed their admiration for the artifacts to the young Picasso and Matisse. Henry Moore contributed a major new direction in sculpture through the influence on his work of the carved Chac-Mools found in pre-Columbian Middle America. And in dance, such innocent imitations as the tarantella in George Balanchine's *Roma* and such potent emulations as the American Indian rites in Martha Graham's *Primitive Mysteries* are significant examples of the ways that tribal rituals shape and vitalize the idiosyncratic rites of artists.

bers

The Alvin Ailey Dance Theater in Donald McKayle's *Blood Memories*.

Graham has made no secret of her debt to the Indians of the Southwest. Barbara Morgan (known for her book *Martha Graham: Sixteen Dances*) made the following remarks in a lecture at the University of Wisconsin: "I had just seen one of Martha's concerts. I can't remember whether it was *Primitive Mysteries or Frontier*, but I was very excited and it aroused memories of my experiences in the Southwest. So I asked Martha very directly, 'By any chance have you been influenced by the Indian and Spanish dance ceremonies in the Southwest?' She said: 'Absolutely, that's one of the greatest inspirations in my entire life.' "

The Kachina Dances

Graham was not the only choreographer to be influenced by the kachina dances of the American Southwest. Erick Hawkins, Lester Horton, Ted Shawn, and José Limón also saw and admired Indian rituals, which had an important impact on their work and that of their students. These ancient Indian rites are still performed today almost identically to their presentation hundreds of years before the arrival of Columbus. They are deeply rooted tribal rituals, and not the intentional "art" of choreographers. They predate the personal rites of artists, but they also lend immense influence to contemporary dance.

These kachina dances, which Graham and several other major choreographers saw in America's Southwestern region, are the public part of an elaborate religious lifestyle. The kachinas of the American Southwest exist in over 250 iconographic forms which are best known to non-Indians in the form of dolls — small painted and decorated figures carved from wood. These dolls are given to Pueblo children so they can learn to identify the various kachinas. The dolls are learning tools, not sacred objects. Once the members of the tribal societies who "impersonate" the kachinas in ceremonial events don their costumes and masks and take up their paraphernalia, they become sacred reflections of the powers of the kachinas; they may not be touched or involved in human conversation or any other form of exchange. The fact that kachinas are sacred doesn't obstruct their potential for actions that are grotesque, outrageous, and highly humorous — all such qualities exist in the great sacred rites of many primal people.

courtesy Smithsonian Institute

An initiation rite for children, admitting the young to the Towami or Kachina society of the Hopi. Walpi Pueblo, Arizona, 1893.

Ritualistic representation is a complex relationship between reality and the symbols used to depict it. In the case of the kachinas the representation is unlike any religious idea of non-Indians. First of all, the kachina of the Pueblo tribes is not a god but a cosmic, ineffable force, existing in three different forms: the first is unseen and unimaginable; the second is the reflection of the kachina power in a human "impersonator" or dancer; and finally, there is the doll which is untouched by the power of the kachina but duplicates its appearance.

In the kachina dances there is no possibility for facile explanations. Nothing can make an "intelligible" experience out of an illogical but meaningful ritual act any more than it is possible to explain a poetic metaphor which exists, in the first place, because it embodies something beyond the grasp of logic. The ritual dramas of the Southwest tell us nothing at the same time as they suggest an entire cosmology to the initiated. Ignoring the world of objective data, which has been

ohn Lindquist

Primal rites transformed into contemporary theater. Here the Jean-Leon Destiné Dance Company performs *La Légende de L'Assotor.*

so explicitly depicted in most Western art and philosophy, the creative power of rituals like the kachina dances lies in their capacity to awaken imagery within us, to compound mystery with more mystery, and to illuminate the unknown without reducing it to the commonplace.

It seems to me that this is the premise of all forms of dance. When it disappears from an idiom of dance, what remains is a form of entertainment rather than art.

Every initiated child of the Southwest tribes knows that the kachinas in the rites are *really* village men dressed up in traditional kilts, paints, feathers, and masks; but this realization doesn't detract in the least from the fact that the kachinas possess great and exceptional powers. The credibility of the kachinas is not based on the acceptance of their actual physical reality any more than the power of a painting requires us to believe that it is something more than paint and canvas. The men who impersonate kachinas are a bit like paintings — merely the physical representation in which something nonphysical is implemented. They are like people in a dream — illogical and unreal as far as waking reality is concerned but absolutely convincing and curiously meaningful while we are dreaming about them.

The rites of the Pueblo tribes arose anonymously from the spiritual life of an entire people and are so complexly interwoven with that people's iconographic values that they have a pervasive depth of meaning for every member of the tribe.

The fundamental process which brought about the kachinas and their many dances is the same as the process — for all its showmanship and superficiality —

Donald McKayle's *Blood Memories,* danced by the Alvin Ailey Dance Company, ritualizes the Afro-American experience.

which brought about Faison's dance *Gazelle.* It is also the force behind the exceptional art of Graham, Hawkins, Alwin Nikolais, Merce Cunningham and — in a curious way — the abstract ballets of George Balanchine.

In the Western world, the arts are conceptually separate. People have come to think of both the practice and the enjoyment of art as the activity of the individual rather than of the group.

Primal people are remote from Western artistic self-consciousness. In primal societies, the arts are aspects of public life which bring together dancing, poetry, and music into a single function: ritual, an all-embracing, often singular, expressive act of a people. As for the "dancers," they simply don't exist. Like the "artist," the professional performer and choreographer are a very recent creation.

Westerners tend to look upon the artist as distinct from the artisan. Even the most hostile critic wouldn't call sculptor Henry Moore a stonemason or Mexican muralist Diego Rivera a house painter. For primal people, the distinction between artist and artisan does not exist. So the specialness of the "artist," as it is understood in the Western world, and the individuality which has become dominant in the white world's view of artistic expressiveness, are alien to tribal peoples, for whom ritual is the pervasive mode of communication and the exclusive form of public expression.

Tribal life is so unified there is simply no need for art to *communicate* anything. It is only when the uniformity of social values in a group begins to shatter that meaning in the arts comes into existence.

Primal peoples are the reservoir of impulse behind dancing. Pearl Primus dances in *Speak to Me of Rivers,* 1944.

The process of individuation and secularization is particularly visible in the history of dance in the Western world. We can clearly see the shift from the mystic acts of tribes to the organized ceremonies of churches, and then the self-serving spectacles which were commissioned by the princes of the Renaissance. We are able to see how the ritual forms of primal people often outlive the spiritual viewpoint they originally contained, and how the motivating forces of dance change from tribal expressiveness to the eccentric creation of an individual choreographer.

In Europe, and especially in Italy, until the middle of the fifteenth century, the Church was virtually the only patron of art, and this largely anonymous art was required to make statements about Catholic beliefs — morality, cosmology, and universal truths. The Renaissance grandees who later dominated the art market had little interest in philosophies, but were inclined to use art to promote their own reputations. Each patron endeavored to commission work which would outshine that sponsored by rivals. It is clear in the relationship between the art of the Church and that of the grandees that the nature and purpose of expressiveness changed drastically. That change is even greater when we consider the transformation of tribal rites into ecclesiastical art. And the most drastic change of all was the transformation of the art created for Renaissance patrons into art produced almost entirely with the motive of self-expression.

The rituals created by individuals have often described a personal vision, but they have also served nationalistic causes. There have been numerous efforts among Black choreographers to reconstruct the African experience — notably in the works of Pearl Primus, but also in the dances of Katherine Dunham, Jean-Leon Destiné, and the choreographers of the Ailey Company. In the years following the Great Depression, choreographers like Anna Sokolow and the New Dance Trio attempted to ritualize their radical political viewpoints. But whether the intention of a choreographer is tribal, social, political, or personal, the process of ritualizing experience is essentially the same. With a historical perspective it is possible to grasp how the competitive flamboyance of the era of Louis XIII of France was central to the formative character of court dancing and ballet. And in more recent times it is clear that the Freudian emphasis upon the interior world influenced the emergence of modern dance and the cult of personality which Isadora Duncan symbolized. This relationship between the driving forces of culture and the forms of dance demonstrates the way in which experience is ritualized. That process is the focus of this book.

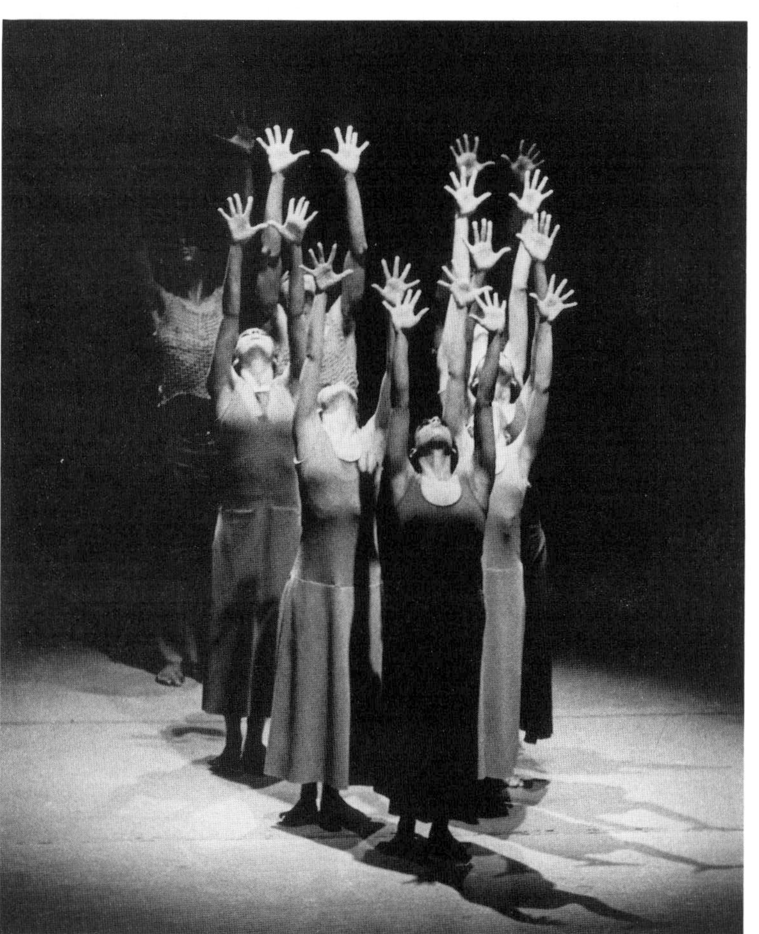
Susan Cook

Company members in Alvin Ailey's Revelations.

The

secret adventures

of order...

—JORGE LUIS BORGES

EXPERIENCE AS RITUAL

AMONG most primal peoples, there is a pantheistic and animistic belief in a world of essences which is embodied in all forces and elements. The name of this fundamental "power" is generally designated in English as *nature*, but a much more accurate term is the word *orenda*, from the Iroquois name for the supernatural energy inherent in everything in the world. The *orendas* of the innumerable beings and objects in the universe, real and "imagined," are greatly different from one another and require different actions for people to remain in a positive relationship with them. Therefore, a great variety of songs and rites must be used in order to maintain a tribe's harmony with this awesome power, which is the absolute basis of everything that exists. Corresponding to the Iroquoian *orenda* is the *wakanda* of the Sioux, the Algonquian *manito*, the Shoshonean *pokunt*, and the Athabascan *coen*. These American Indian words cannot be translated into any non-Indian language. They represent a concept so fundamentally different from the worldview of Westerners that an involved discussion is required merely to touch upon their significance — something which anthropologist Carlos Castaneda has perceptively called "a separate reality" in his tetralogy on the Yaqui Indian teacher Don Juan.

Some inkling of the awesomeness of the *orendas* can be grasped when we encounter the way in which Indians act out their worldview in rituals. If you agree with those who believe that action came before conjecture in human development, then you will recognize in bodily movement humanity's most fundamental and expressive act. It is the inclination of primal peoples to idealize action as a magical force. There is substantial physiological basis behind this ancient idea.

Isadora Duncan, dancing amoung the Greek ruins in 1904, rediscovers the articulate body.

We are born with organs of perception that provide us with our only means of experiencing the world. These organs include not only the sense of smell, sight, hearing, taste, and touch, but also a sense of balance and of rotation, which the semicircular canals in the inner ear reveal to us. In addition, we possess a kinesthetic sense, operating through receptors in our muscle tissue and through our tactual sensitivity to pressure and texture, which helps us realize when we are moving and on what kind of surface. From birth we are taught to recognize the ways in which the movements of our bodies work practically for us: eating, swimming, driving, typing, writing. Bodily movement has other functions, however, and primal people are as aware of them as they are of the purely practical ways in which motion serves them. Every emotional state expresses itself in movements that are not necessarily utilitarian or representational, but that nevertheless reflect the specific quality of the experience that causes them. The term "emotional state," in the context of fundamental feelings, is perhaps less accurate than the word "sentience," since I am talking about something other than rampant emotion. The relationship between sentience and movement affects everything from the expression in our eyes to the flow of adrenalin in our bodies. In its most fundamental form, this spontaneous link between mentality, feeling, and movement is called dance — a direct, nonverbal, unreasoned assertion of sentience (the mergence of thought and feeling) in universal forms of pure physical assertion. Dance is clearly an extremely powerful force in human experience, especially if we live in a society in which less importance is given to words than to actions (which is particularly the case among people with an oral rather than a written tradition).

Beyond the purely expressive powers of movement there is also its highly contagious nature. Yawning is the most obvious example of this; so is the desire to stretch when we see someone else stretching. Because of the inherent contagion of motion, which makes the onlooker feel in his own body the exertion he sees in others, the dancer is able to convey nonverbally, even nonsymbolically, the most intangible experiences, ideas, and feelings.

The body is capable of communicating in its own bodily manner. When one considers how powerfully movement influences us, it isn't difficult to understand why primal people regard an action as the embodiment of a mysterious force. They believe that dance can shape the circumstances of nature if it can focus its contagious power on animals and supernaturals. This premise of sympathetic magic is at the root of most ceremonial use of dance. The imitation of an animal (essentially in movements, but also in costume) has an influence on the animal itself. This practice, called homeopathic ritual, is the basis of most hunting and fertility rites. It probably resulted from a long history of less complex usages of bodily motion until it was determined that actions of a certain kind were effective: depicting the pursuit and slaying of an animal might assure success in the hunt, etc. At such a point, thought and action are fused in a form almost unknown in civilization except, perhaps, in the specialized process which is separated from the practical activities of life and called "art."

In the fusion of dance, song, and music among primal people, we discover "art" before art consciously exists for them. In most primal languages there is no equivalent of the West's notion of art. The purpose of most ritual art is curiously ambiguous at the same time that it seems to be practical from the Western standpoint. The Navajo *Night Chant*, for instance, is a ritual concerned with a curative procedure enacted by a holy man ("chanter") to remedy the ills of a tribesman ("patient"). But in the use of the word "patient" (which applies to the person who pays for the performance of the rite) the significance of the illness from the Navajo viewpoint is entirely lost. The "disease" to be cured is an ailment of the "spiritual body," which has mysteriously lost touch with the universe. The idea that spirituality can be associated with the body is extremely remote from the Western belief in the dichotomy of mind and body, spirit and flesh. It was until very recently inconceivable in the world of Christians and Jews that there could be any relationship between spiritual and physical reality.

It was not until the turn of this century that dance was evolved into a real art form by people like Isadora Duncan and Loie Fuller. Until then, body movement possessed a humble and static existence in Western civilization. It was so detested by both the church and the synagogue that it was officially prohibited after a brief but important expressive use in early religious ceremo-

courtesy Library of Congress

Founding a school of American dancing — Isadora Duncan and the Isadorables.

uthor's collection

The Ted Shawn Men's Group, finding a new place for males in dance, performs "Earth" from *Dances of the Ages*. 1938.

nies. It is difficult, after centuries of belief in the mortification of the flesh (and the celebration of the disembodied soul), for most Westerners to grasp the possibility of a "spiritual body" in which spirit and flesh are united, in which feeling and thought are unified. The American Indian concept of harmony among all things is so alien to the West that people cannot conceive of a spiritual conviction that can be communicated through dance — a unique expressive act in which, more than any other, there is immediacy and a perfect mergence of idea and feeling. It is a predicament of Western civilization perhaps brought about by the intellectual idea of Europeans to dominate, predict, and change nature. American Indians, particularly, and most other primal peoples, envision life as harmonious with nature. To primal peoples the world does not consist of inanimate materials and living things; *everything* is living and everything can, therefore, be of help or cause harm. That is the basis for the ritual relationship of primal people and nature. They have none of the cosmic egotism of Western civilization which sees humanity as the crowning achievement of evolution.

In their effort to move closer to the centers of power in nature, primal people often imitate and transform themselves into things of the natural world that invest them with strength and vision. They receive power through their songs. Through dances they touch unknown and unseen elements, which they sense in the world around them. It is perhaps an error to speak of the *imitation* of animals, because human actions are really designed not for emulation but for transformation. Modern dancers have consciously rediscovered this same process: they do not simply *perform* the movements of a choreographer — they *become* the movements, through intense kinesthetic projection of ideas and feeling as pure bodily expression. It is a process difficult to describe as it takes place in tribal rites, but it is essential to the nature of dance as an expressive, nondecorative form. When we see this process in a work by Erick Hawkins or Meredith Monk, we are at a loss to describe how it happens. For primal peoples, this process of being transformed into movement is easy. "To you," they explain, "the apple is a very, very complicated and mysterious thing. But for the apple tree it is easy."

Ideas and feelings are merged in the spiritual body. Words — chanted, sung, or spoken — are valued in rituals primarily for the reaction they produce within the singer rather than for any effect they might have on others. The first stage of ritual is almost always the rise of the singer on his or her own song to a plane of power — a place of contact with the forces that move the universe. The words and sounds of a song are only the small visible aspect of a far greater mystery which lies beneath and beyond syntactical speech. For this reason, the nature of ritual songs requires the comprehension of a larger idea, a sound of a word or two that conveys something wider and truer than what is actually spoken.

No one knows for certain just how song and dance originated. But there is in all animals, including humans, a relationship between intense feeling and involuntary bodily movement and utterance. Due to the stresses of movement upon the solar plexus and upon the diaphragm, there is a tendency for vocalization. It is the kind of noise people make when they sit down or get up, or when they are surprised or dismayed. The contractive movement of many ritual dances also results in the forced exhalation of breath, thus causing vocalization. The variety of movement, accent, and intensity produce many different sounds. It is possible that some of the songs which accompany dance are the results of such utterances, which involuntarily occur during dancing. Whatever the origin of song and its relationship to dance, we know from ethnologists that song and dance are intrinsic in most primal cultures — the dancers accompany themselves with sounds of rhythmic accents produced by clapping and stomping. It is often conjectured that once the energies of the dance accelerated, making self-accompaniment difficult, the beat and vocal sounds were picked up by a less active dancer or bystanders who eventually became the "orchestra." In this way, dance emerged as a distinct form from music in the ritual arts.

The outward rusticity of primal behavior makes Western people devise a self-serving ideal of themselves as *civilized*, which widely separates them from other people. They are inclined to forget that the same impulses which give form to primal people are active in all cultures despite apparent diversity. Twentieth-century people are products of their gradual withdrawal from an awareness of nature and their place in it. They believe that nature serves them and that divine intention makes them the dominant being of the world. In contrast, primal people live among animals and vegetation, constantly in close contact with the sources of nourishment and death, understanding their environment and expressing their ideas and their feelings in terms of the natural world, rather than some curiously unnatural idealization they have constructed about themselves in relation to the world.

The response of primal people to their environment is largely ritualistic...an idealization of the relationship of human beings to their surroundings. Modern people, however, often try to neutralize (rather than to ritualize) their experience of nature. Ritual tends to deal with ambiguity on the level of ambiguity — in the way that art deals with reality. On the other hand, the "civilized" viewpoint is inclined to turn ambiguity into certitude and orthodoxy. The central method for this transposition from a world of essences to a world of objects, as philosophers Ernst Cassirer and Susanne Langer have indicated, is through the use of words as the definitive framework of realism. "Words are certainly our most important instruments of expression," Langer informs us in *Philosophy in a New Key,* "our most characteristic, universal and enviable tools in the conduct of life. Speech is the mark of humanity. It is the normal terminus of thought. We are apt to be so impressed with its symbolistic mission that we regard it as the only important expressive act, and assume that all other activity must be practical in an animalian way, or else irrational — playful, or atavistic (residual) past recognition. But in fact, speech is the natural outcome of only one kind of symbolic process. There are transformations of experience in the human mind that have quite different overt endings. They end in acts that are neither practical nor communicative, though they may be both effective and communal; I mean the actions we call *ritual.*"

Ritual is a symbolic transformation of experiences which no other medium of expression can adequately contain. Because it springs from a primary human need, it is a spontaneous activity that arises without self-consciousness, without adaptation to either a pragmatic or conscious purpose. Its growth is undesigned in the sense that primal architecture is "undesigned." Its patterns, for all their intricacy, merely express the social process of a unique people who are largely unconscious of the social structure in which they live. Ritual is never successfully imposed on a people. When such missionary efforts are made, the imposed ideology is thoroughly assimilated into preexisting ritual forms.

The province of ritual, like dance, has been continually assaulted as mindless and compulsive because it does not sustain the certitude and orthodoxy of the language-bound mentality of civilized people. Freud saw rites as acts which must be performed out of sheer inward need. It is now apparent that ritual acts are often the spontaneous transformation of external as well as internal experience. A good example of ritual as a form of social accommodation is visible in the *Booger Dance* of the Big Cove band of the Eastern Cherokees. In this ritual, which is not quite the same as any other Cherokee ceremony, we discover a dramatic record of the anxiety of the tribe, a strong reaction against the symbol of the white invaders, and an expression of fear in dealing with the white world that surrounds the Big Cove settlement. The *Booger Dance* fuses the invasion of the white man to the spiritual forces of nature with which the Cherokee had learned to cope, therefore making the existence of whites somehow less alien and threatening. The Cherokee believe that they cannot politically deal with the white invaders, but feel completely competent to cope with the same white people transformed by ritual into mythical animals and grotesquely obscene creatures which invade the Indian settlement in a ritual performance. In other words, the Indians do not feel sufficiently powerful politically and pragmatically to deal with white people. They do, however, feel competent to do so through ritual — the means by which, at a much earlier time, they successfully transmuted their very harsh geographical environment into a familiar ritual context through which they could assert influence and with which they could ultimately achieve harmony.

The *Booger Dance* perfectly ritualizes an ugly and difficult experience for the Cherokee Indians. It describes the coming of outsiders, who are changed into the Boogers, who intrude in the midst of tribal life uninvited, seeking something to exploit. In the dance, the Indians tolerate the invaders until, their desires gratified, the whites leave. Thus the white man's existence, his unmannerly insistences, and his intrusion into the Cherokee home circle at the height of social festivities become grotesque and comic aspects of a ritual experience. But the ritual does not indulge in wishful thinking. The whites are realistically depicted as successfully aggressive and dominant intruders, but these characteristics are transformed into grotesque parody. The Boogers have obscene names and wear imitation sex organs made of gourds, which are filled with water that sprays in every direction as they chase Indian women. When the Boogers are asked what they want, they at first say "Girls!" Told politely that Indian women do not like Boogers, they then say they want "to fight!" The Cherokee leader explains that Indians are peaceful and do not want to fight but that they are willing to dance with the Boogers. The invaders accept the invitation to dance and use the opportunity to abuse the native women who join them in the dance but who remain aloof from the Boogers' simulation of sexual aggression. Then the Boogers depart, having been successfully neutralized by this ritual. The Cherokees celebrate their cultural victory over those who defeated them militaristically.

The *Booger Dance* contradicts much of what Freud and his followers have assumed about ritual acts. These acts are not necessarily unconscious outpourings of feelings into shouting, prancing, and rolling on the ground, like a baby's tantrum. For as soon as an expressive act is intentionally performed without compulsion, it is no longer "self-expressive," in the narrow, psychopathic sense. Instead, it becomes logically expressive, but not necessarily in the kind of logic conveyed by words. Neither is the *Booger Dance* simply a set of emotional *signs*; rather it is a symbol for an *entire* experience. Instead of completing the natural history of emotions, the dance denotes feelings and ambiguously summons these feelings to mind without actuating them.

If the *Booger Dance* of the Cherokee Indians is repeatedly performed for the sheer joy of expression, it becomes aesthetic at that point. Anger enjoyed in being acted out consciously is not mere compulsive anger. The ultimate product of such articulation of tensions is not a simple emotion, but a complex and relatively permanent attitude which expresses itself through a variety of forms typical of the culture which produces it. As it develops toward an aesthetic character, ritual expresses feelings and ideas in the formal rather than the purely physiological sense. The word *expression*, as I use it here in relation to ritual and dance, is a deliberate conveyance of values — and not simply an emotional outburst or a public tantrum.

author's collection

The imitation of exotic cultures was a preoccupation of Ted Shawn and Ruth St. Denis before their discovery of American roots.

The process of civilization may be contradictory to the process of art and ritual. In civilization, the power of these activities is gradually displaced and abandoned as people discover cause and effect and pursue the control of nature by methods which alter the causal circumstances of their existence. At such a time, the power of actions and images ceases to be a prime object of the community. Dance persists, but it expresses itself on the basis of other aims and principles. In southern France, for instance, a folk dance called the farandole is still performed. It is a labyrinth-patterned dance common in much folk choreography. Its patterns derive from an ancient symbol found on Greek coins.

The snakelike winding of the farandole of Provence, an ancient colony of Greece, closely resembles a journey to the middle of a labyrinth. This Greek labyrinth pattern was a vision of the passage of a dead man to the land of the afterlife, a passage fraught with danger from evil powers. In performing a funeral dance toward the middle of a man-made labyrinth, the ancients were de-

author's collection

Ruth St. Denis and Ted Shawn in "Tillers of the Soil" from *Dance Pageant of Egypt, Greece and India,* 1916.

monstrating that humans possess the force to direct certain events of nature through sympathetic rites. This winding farandole was a means of mimicking the spirit of the dead man and helping him on his way. Today, the farmers of Provence still perform the farandole, but without much purpose other than the enjoyment of music and movement. In this case, the expressive form of the ritual has been abandoned. What remains is neither art nor ritual but something else: an entertainment, a game. It is possible, in this context, that much of what has normally been called "dance" is likewise neither art nor ritual but decorative entertainment.

The rituals of primal people are products of hundreds of generations, a slow selective process by which certain actions are retained through repetition. These rites possess strong magic. They do not easily vanish and leave only a game (a seemingly purposeless pattern of exuberant physical movements) except under specific duress and over a great period of time. Sooner or later in the forward push of civilization toward a totally controlled and verbalized construct of nature, a mimetic dance form appears which exists as a dumb show, a substitution for words. Out of this pragmatic dance comes the separation of drama, dance, and music. Ultimately, not only power and expressivity but also dance movement itself pass from the rituals of civilization, and a purely narrative mime of ideas comes into existence. This is the basis of naïve realism.

Dance is often viewed as a decorative residue which, without drama or music, has no basis for existence except as mindless frivolity and as an excuse for exhibiting flamboyant costumes and decor. In the gender-stereotyping of Western civilization, dance is also reduced to the sentimental and unthinking "world of women," making it unfit for male participation and unsuited for any female who hopes to escape the narrowness of sexual stereotypes. It is little wonder that, for generations, dance in the university has been pushed from the women's physical education department to the music department and the school of drama without often establishing its own prerogative. In most American cities, music critics are required to review dance events as well. It's an unreasonable situation, since most of them don't know anything about dance. They see the relationship between music and choreography as "music visualization," in which the dancers are used like props out of *Fantasia* — going up when the music goes up and bourréeing through clouds to the accompaniment of tiptoe music. That is the best reaction you can expect from most music critics at a dance program. They believe dance is essentially a series of Frenchified acrobatics contrived with enough zeal to distract the audience from an otherwise horrendous piece of music. Almost any music critic will tell you that if the music were really good, nobody would have to dance to it.

Nothing prepares most music critics for the uniqueness of dance. The character of opera and other forms of theatrical music is largely built on embroidery: using decor to illustrate a form of theater still heavily anchored to the realism of the turn of the century. Music critics do not generally realize that dance is able to ritualize experience in a way that fuses music and motion. It is an ancient and largely lost form which has been dissipated ever since song, dance, and prayer became separate actions.

The Ineffable "Thing" Itself

History used to be considered a relentless development toward perfection. No longer. Nothing changes as drastically as the value system by which we judge progress unless it is the values we attach to emotions. Feelings and the things which evoke them are constantly coming in and going out of fashion. Shakespeare's audience wept for Romeo. One hundred years later, the Restoration audience of William Congreve was laughing at seduction and rape. A mere fifty years passed, and Balzac succeeded in sentimentalizing seduction with his invention of the whore with the heart of gold. It was not too many years before Sigmund Freud totally reshaped our attitude about love by suggesting that it was something in need of a "cure."

"Art must be recognized as the most certain mode of expression which mankind has achieved," Herbert Read has stated in *Art and Society*. "As such it has been propagated from the very dawn of civilization. In every age man has made things for use and followed thousands of occupations made necessary by his struggle for existence. He has fought endlessly for power and leisure and for material happiness. He has created languages and symbols and built up an impressive fund of learning; his resources and inventions have never been exhausted. And yet all the time, in every phase of civilization, he has felt that what we call the scientific attitude is inadequate. The mind he has developed from his deliberate cunning can only cope with objective facts; beyond these objective facts is a whole aspect of the world which is only accessible to intuition. The development of these obscure modes of apprehension has been the purpose of art; and we are nowhere near an understanding of mankind until we admit the significance and indeed the superiority of such knowledge because whilst nothing has proved so impermanent and provisional as that which we are pleased to call scientific fact and the whole philosophy built on it, art, on the contrary, is everywhere, in its highest manifestations, both universal and external."

I was once given advice by an old man. "You must learn to look at the world twice," he told me as I sat on the floor of his immaculately swept adobe room. "First you must bring your eyes together in front so you can see each droplet of rain on the grass, so you can see the smoke rising from an anthill in the sunshine. *Nothing* should escape your notice. But you must learn to look again, with your eyes at the very edge of what is visible. Now you must see dimly if you wish to see things that are dim — visions, mist, and cloud-people...animals which hurry past you in the dark. You must learn to look at the world twice if you wish to see all that there is to see."

The ability to envision a second world is a major source of ritual knowledge — that which is so deeply known and felt, so primal in form that it is neither word not outcry, neither sign nor symbol, but the ineffable *thing* itself, that which precedes speech and thought, that which is the raw experience itself without evaluation or moralities. It is the ineffable, structured into an event — that which is called *ritual*. And what, after all, is this mysterious event that has eluded the Western mind, and why have I spent so much time discussing it as a prerequisite for understanding dance? It is an appearance — an apparition, if you like — that springs not from what we are but from what we do. It is something else. In watching a ritual, or a dance, you do not see what is physically before you. What you see is an interaction of forces by which something else arises. Those who see only what is before them are blind. Ritual, like dance, requires us to *really* see. What we are able to see if we use our bodies as eyes is a virtual image. It is real, for when we are confronted by it, it really does exist, but it is not actually there. The reflection in a mirror is such a virtual image; so is a rainbow. It seems to stand on earth or in the clouds, but it really "stands" nowhere. It is only visible, not tangible. It is the unspeakable, the ineffable made visible, made audible, made experiential.

If we can accept the paradox that our essential humanity is understood through our cultural differences rather than our cultural similarities, then it is possible that the ritual life of primal peoples embodies an enduring and luminous insight into something so fundamentally human that many of us have lost track of it in our devastating lessons of uniformity and equality. At the core of everyone's culture is a package of beliefs which every child learns and which has been culturally determined long in advance of his or her birth. The world is rendered coherent by our description of it. What we see when we speak of reality is simply

that preconception. At the core of Western experience is a condition of culture which insists blindly that what is described as truth is absolute, whereas at the core of primal people's viewpoint is usually the assumption that reality is not an absolute. They experience many separate realities. They believe in a multi-verse, or a biverse, but not the uni-verse of Western civilization.

This singularity of the cosmos is a conviction of the dominant group with which, as Herbert Read has said, it seems persistently uncomfortable. Ever since the ecstatic mystery rites of pre-Socratic Greece declined, Western civilization has been continually challenged by its dream of escaping its own framework: the categorical, the linear, and the eternally fixed and knowable. The forward plunge of civilization, which some look upon as progress, has brought the impulse to express feelings too rigidly under the domination of reason, and this, in turn, has caused many Western people to think of themselves predominantly as perpetual spectators of the world, afraid to create their own forms because they might fall outside the conventional preconception of reality. Until very recently, most white people were cut off from their own bodies and from expressive activities by their own constraint and embarrassment. They lacked a body that could function in harmony with their ideas and feelings. Consequently they were reassured of the old Christian assessment of the body as a liability and as a humble organism over which they possessed little control. Without an *articulate body*, without facial movement which genuinely reflects states of mind, without a torso which responds to the self and relates to external events, people cannot participate in their world or in their own emotional lives.

The perfectly coordinated, lavishly expressive body of the ritual dancer is unmistakably different from the prim, stiff, and fashionably prancing body of the ballet dancer. In the ceremonial performer, there is an idealized transparency—a configuration in which the totality of human experience is visible. The feelings intrinsic to ritual are probably no more fundamental or primitive than the loftiest sentience of any of the Western arts. The ideas inherent in ritual dancing may appear at first simplistic because white people, at least until Isadora Duncan, did not believe that something as inarticulate and fanciful as dance could possibly convey anything profound. That is perhaps true of European dance, which had greatly declined from its ritual purposes when contemporary dancers at the turn of the century began the arduous effort of rediscovering the potential of relating dancing to the most serious rather than the most superficial aspects of the human condition. But for primal peoples, dance perfectly and simultaneously embodies the most commonplace and the most exceptional ideas. If dance relates imperfectly to the contemporary world, and if choreographers have found it difficult to invest movement with an awareness of the feelings and ideas that have evolved in the West for centuries, it is perhaps because dance was so neglected during that long evolution and did not develop the kind of relationship to the white audience which it has always had in relation to primal cultures.

Martha Graham once said that dance is stupendously simple, and that that is what makes it so difficult for modern man to comprehend. The idea of the spiritual body is equally simple. If there were better words to describe such a

uth St. Denis, eighty years old, in "Black and Gold Sari," oward the end of the first generation of American nodern dance.

phenomenon, perhaps it would be easier to articulate this idea, but in that case it would be doubtful that there would be any reason to talk about ritual, ceremony, and dance in the first place. There is nothing really spiritual in the concept of the spiritual body, but there isn't another word that suggests all the qualities of nobility, loftiness of thought, intensity of ideals and feelings which we normally exclude from our connotation of *body*. The concept behind the term "spiritual body" does not envision just the anatomical body but all the still-mysterious physiology by which the body experiences itself and the world, the amplification of the senses and the puzzling process of perception and thought by which "brain" recreates itself as "mind."

A body is all there is of us, whether we believe that our existence is wholly material or not. Primal people have little faith in the materialism that begs the question of mind/brain or soul/body. The primal process of life is holistic and formative. It is not imprisoned in a *universe* with its compulsive axioms concerning a whole greater than the sum of its parts, but with an imagination that can deal only with the parts, never the whole. So-called primitives are not stuck with one truth, one god, one universe and one ultimate equation by which *everything* — which no one grasps anyway — operates, moving the gears of the vast, unthinkable Copernican cosmos like some pathetic clock by which only civilized whites are supposed to be able to tell the correct time.

The story of dance in the Western world is as much an alternative vision of the events of history as is the folk history told for generations by primal people. Both white and nonwhite dancers for all their differences seem to have something in common: they are both aliens standing outside the value systems of the dominant culture. The changes in viewpoint since the turn of the century are connected with the current dance boom. A reappraisal of sex roles, of ethnocentricity, of civilization, and of the human community have vitally altered white people's attitudes toward themselves and their bodies.

It is an ideal time to introduce a vision of the history of dance which arises from a primal/folk consciousness — and to re-examine the world of dance in terms alien to the preconceptions of civilization. "No form of dance is permanent," critic John Martin observed. "No form of dance is definitive, ultimate... only the basic principle of dance is enduring, and out of it, like the cycle of nature itself, rises an endless succession of new springs out of old winters."

The resurrection of Isadora — Lynn Seymour in *Five Waltzes in the Manner of Isadora Duncan* at the American Ballet Theatre Gala, 1970.

N.Y. Public Library Picture Collection

Eleven maenads dancing to flute music seen in a painting on the inside of Greek eating vessel.

I am a brother
to dragons,
and a companion
to owls.

—JOB 30:29

HISTORY AS RITUAL

"WHATEVER the nature of dance," the critic Curt Sachs once wrote, "it needs no onlooker, not even a single witness. Nevertheless, in spite of its ecstatic and liturgical character, there early appears the germ of that great process of change which has gradually transformed the dance from an involuntary motor discharge, and a ceremonial rite, into a work of art conscious of and intended for observation."

It is also likely that the momentum which brought about the transformation of ritual into a form intended for spectators stemmed from the religious necessity for correctness in ritual acts. In the New Hebrides, any dancer making a mistake was assaulted, wounded, and possibly killed by bowmen posted to keep careful watch for inaccuracies in rituals. By the time the cultures of Egypt and the Far East arose, ritual had been replaced in many regions by *ceremony*. Ceremony was a highly planned, structured, and precise form which demanded the instruction of priests in order to faithfully adhere to tradition. Every error decreased the power and efficacy of the ceremonial act. Exactitude and formality, rather than spontaneity and expressiveness, became the premise of this newly evolved ceremonial activity. Of course, the process was not abrupt: rituals had always possessed some degree of formality. By using the term "ceremony," however, I am describing the transition from participation by a tribe in ritualistic expression to the ceremonial formality of a priestly caste, which tended to exclude the impulse that had originally given rise to ritual. If it were not for the ever-refining preoccupation of religion and the traditions of its exclusive and secretive priest caste, dance might have remained a purely expressional phenomenon—a complex extension of animal impulses. We shall never know.

Ancient Egypt, Wilkenson

Two male Egyptian dancers face each other in a typical ancient dance, advancing, withdrawing and concluding by turning each other around.

The first civilizations were intent upon monumentality: massive architecture, the accumulation of wealth, and geographical expansion. The world which emerges in the chronicles of the time is very different from the world of prehistory we can envision from the residue of ritual forms.

Nomadic life was a memory for the groups of people who founded and populated the cultures which have left powerful and flamboyant impressions on history. Unfortunately, history is always the story of dominant peoples and rarely makes reference to minorities except in taking note of them as "barbarian invaders" who occasionally press upon the boundaries of "civilization."

It is important, however, to recognize a fact that does not make any appearance in history books: primal activities, including dance, always continued to exist beyond the borders of civilizations, untouched and largely unchanged by the surrounding concentration of mechanical progress and technology. Considering the many centuries humanity has been able to assert influence on a worldwide basis, it is astounding how aloof and isolated primal groups have remained from the so-called mainstream of human development. These "barbarians" unwittingly retained much of the fundamental character of ritual and dance. Meanwhile, civilization transformed dance into a ceremonial form focused upon literal ideas.

Egypt, Greece, and, later, Rome were concerned with the organization of a social-political structure in which divinity served humanity rather than the reverse. Spiritual life had become a conscious form of political action. Animism and pantheism with their innumerable fetishes and totems were considered primitive and crude. *Power* was no longer praised in nature but in a hierarchy of priests, priest-kings, and god-kings. Human sensibility had undergone a peculiar change: as language had grown more and more to embrace abstractions the mentality of humans had become increasingly logical and positivist. As the speciality of language increased so did verbal exactitude. Ideas were now contained within the framework of a limited and fixed series of signs. But language not only permits us to communicate; it also limits what we can think and what we can convey to each other. The "poetic" ambiguity of primal people was therefore exchanged for an orderly occultism.

When the high priest of Egypt danced the role of the god Osiris in a great religious drama connected with the flooding of the Nile Valley, we easily recognize the sympathetic magic of primal people in his activity: he attempted to gain control over something by pretending to be it. We can also recognize that the magical object had drastically changed into a deliberate, anthropomorphic idea. The human character of Osiris changed the *power* that primal people had seen *in nature* into the *divinity* which civilized people saw *in themselves*. Prayer was largely based upon political diplomacy: praise of, and humiliation before, an apparently highly egocentric potentate. The human nature of Osiris provided an easy premise for the creation of ceremonial procedures: persuasions of wealth or sacrifices of a more bloody nature could sweep aside his discontents and bring him egotistical satisfaction. Whereas ritual had dealt with the unknown in terms of the unknown, ceremony dealt with it in terms of the commonplace. What makes this basic alteration in human expressiveness important here is the fact that it provided a new framework for dancing.

For one thing, dancing became a profession consisting mainly of men, though it also had its minority of female exponents who eventually developed into a caste of "temple harlots" (a paradoxical embodiment of both virgin and fertility goddess). In Egypt, none of the numerous dance pictures, and none of the hieroglyphic records, reveal any form of true social dancing. The aristocratic Egyptian, in other words, didn't join in any form of choral dance. There seems to have been no form of dance for couples and no solo dance, except for the performances by ceremonial dancers and entertainers. But the peasantry — those who had largely

Greek dancers from a fourth century B.C. kylix.

courtesy of British Museum, London

courtesy Metropolitan Museum of Art

Etruscan dancers from a wall painting of the fifth century B.C.

escaped the restraints of civilization — continued to celebrate the ancient rituals. For instance, a harvest dance is depicted in relief in a tomb from the fifth dynasty of Giza, about 2700 B.C., which is clearly a residue of peasant ritual.

Once secularization and specialization had introduced art and dance as the occupation of professionals, people developed a consciousness of technique and aesthetic values. Dance was no longer a spontaneous or improvisational activity except among the peasantry. The professionalization of dancing brought about a complex technique which was beyond the capacity of nonprofessionals and excluded their participation. Such technicality produced both restriction and experimentation. And eventually the purely secular dance, invested with athleticism and playfulness, made its appearance in the houses of lords as a form of entertainment.

We do not know how the ancient Greeks danced. Of the 95,140 combined body movements which have been laboriously calculated to have existed in their dances; we still haven't the vaguest idea how they looked in action. But we do know some of the reasons why the Greeks danced, and that perhaps is more important than how they danced. A romanticized picture of Greek dance has served as a model for several eras. The court dancers of the Renaissance, who evolved into ballet dancers, obviously did not understand Greek culture, though it gave impetus to the entire rebirth of Western art. Much later, Isadora Duncan also failed to recreate the dances of Greece despite her enthusiasm for the Hellenic world.

Yet, by some quirk of intuition Duncan may have grasped much of the motive behind Greek dancing. In the ancient world a prominent matriarchal concept had persisted, undoubtedly due to the racial and cultural origins of those peoples who migrated from the north to conquer the Minoan and Mycenaean societies and to become the Greeks. Without dredging up the vast anthropological evidence for this matriarchal notion, which began with Robert Briffault in the nineteenth century and culminates in the works of the feminists, it is not unlikely that much of what we consider as the aesthetic refinement and humanism of Greece was directly related to the influences of a moribund matriarchy which was barely visible at the outset of recorded history.

The world which Isadora hoped to emulate was a world strongly directed by the residue of a matriarchal-agricultural period far behind it in time — so far behind, as a matter of fact, that women were cast in a low state in Greece, though testimony of their majesty was everywhere visible in the hierarchy of the gods, in the epics, and in the great dramas. These ancient expressions of a Greek matriarchy had arisen from a primal reservoir: from animal ancestry and nature spirits and from a powerful humanism which gave meaning and value to life. The development of the famous dramatic dithyrambs of the Dionysian dancers represents perhaps the highest level of ceremonial art — a level where fundamentals of human realism are glorified, rather than buried beneath the stress of materialism. It is significant that the development of Greek classical theater from an ancient fertility ritual was achieved without the destruction of those values intrinsic to such a ritual. It is possible, of course, that this idealization of Greek drama as a true ritual form comes from the fact that the West is an extension of Greek civilization, but it remains that in the Western world we find much of our humanity fulfilled in the perfection of Hellenic drama with its eloquent choral dances and distant vision of a world still imbued with mystery and power.

Rome, on the other hand, was not interested in mystery, but solely in power. "No sober person dances," Cicero wrote with great authority, perfectly epitomizing the Roman world of political science, jurisprudence, and oratory. The rudest element of this legacy from Rome is the contention that anything of value can be expressed in words or it is not worth expressing at all. "Words," Cicero stated, "possess meaning. If something cannot be said in words, it has no meaning." This is still a central axiom of Western civilization.

While the Greeks were concerned with the exclusiveness of city-states, the Romans were interested in an inclusive imperialism which bred contempt for humanity, a mercenary view of culture, and an all-absorbing concern for the material needs of maintaining a vast empire: roads, service organizations, military systems, and accelerated agricultural production.

Rome did not invent indulgence; its free-for-all holiday Saturnalia was the political expression of an ancient ritual. But that national holiday, with its unrestrained license, helped to epitomize the Roman view of the body and of dance as an expression of sexual hedonism. Sexuality is always associated with dancing by materialistic people. Lucian summed up the Roman view of dance: "The dancer's

author's collection

Roman masked performers dance to their own music in a comic theatrical scene depicted in a mosaic from Pompeii.

principal task is to imitate, and to show forth his subject by means of gesticulation. He, like the orators, must acquire lucidity; every scene must be intelligible without the aid of an interpreter; to borrow the expression of the Pythian oracle 'Dumb though he be, and speechless, he is heard!'"

This succession of cultures produced a succession of dance forms. Not only did the external shapes and steps of various dances change, but so did the innermost motives which gave rise to the fundamental reason for dancing. Ritual as a tribal, expressive form of people's relationship to the power of nature had evolved into a ceremonial art in which the confines of language turned the ineffable into a logical, systematic, formalistic reflection of humanity itself. The intrusion of syntax upon imagination continued. Its triumph was the pantomimic art of Rome. The dance of primal ecstasy was sexualized by the Roman mentality and became the first form of intentionally lewd cabaret entertainment. The dance of Rome brought the temple harlot down from her special place among the priests into the marketplace, defaming both dance and religion.

The classical era closed upon a social structure dying of the wounds of realism. While an infinitely small portion of people were participating in the rise and fall of civilizations, the vast majority of people continued on their traditional, ritualistic course. In much of western Europe, in Africa and parts of Asia, in the Americas, Australia and the Pacific Islands the people were still surrounded by first principles beyond their grasp. Gradually the folk population had evolved a greater and greater diversity of cultural forms. By the time of the collapse of Rome, primal art had reached a definitive and highly evolved state. This art was to remain a rich reservoir of human values for almost two thousand years before its impact resurfaced in the arts of the twentieth century.

The Rites of Power and Peasantry

The power of Rome was so fabulous that it asserted its influence over people who had never even encountered a Roman. Though the political center of the empire was more distant to medieval folk than the planets are for us today, its enthralling fables of power were everywhere. Lactantius wrote: "When Rome, the head of the world, shall have fallen, who can doubt that the end is done of human things, aye, of the earth itself?" For many years after the fall of Rome, Christians in remote regions assumed that the empire was still strong — for, indeed, the world had not yet ended. And when Charlemagne established a new Frankish realm in the West, people believed that he had not created anything new — he had merely restored the Roman Empire to its proper realm of power. Such was the characteristic naïveté of the Middle Ages.

The people of the scattered political princedoms saw a world more confined and narrow than that of the seafaring Greeks, who were citizens of proud city-states. The medieval population stood in awe of the venerable tradition which they had inherited, for their own world was largely primitive and exceedingly remote from the greatness which they saw glimmering in the distance where vast imperial cities were rumored to exist.

The people of the Middle Ages adored gaudy colors and spectacles, fighting and adventure, fantasy and romance. They made up elaborate rules for everything and obeyed them very solemnly (while the inspiration lasted). Then, they moved on to other things. They transformed their great Roman-Christian heritage with

The Egg Dance was a peasant entertainment of the Middle Ages.

author's collection

a boundless imaginativeness, magnifying its most wondrous and fearsome aspects. They also played at life, indulging the grotesque fancy and mischievous humor that adorned their cathedrals with leering gargoyles. They were as ingenious in piety as in blasphemy. The central motif of the Middle Ages was perpetual paradoxy: a religious dogma insistent upon moderation, embraced with total abandon.

Philip the Good was a typical medieval personality, famous for both the number of his bastards and the austerity of his fasts. "At no time in the world's history," concluded historian James Bryce, "has theory, professing all the while to control practice, been so utterly divorced from it." For instance, there were elaborate ceremonies in which the people of the Middle Ages could renounce vanity with great flamboyance and pomp. Their high sense of honor, a blend of fine conscience and rude egotism, enabled them to set up an ideal of selfless fidelity, to seek personal glory, to gratify their love of fighting, to maintain standards of justice, and to wreak a barbarous vengeance on their enemies. The great cathedrals were favorite trysting places for young lovers and a hunting ground for prostitutes. Students had to be continually discouraged from playing dice on the altars of Notre Dame by threats of excommunication. Sexuality was implicit in the idea of religious ecstasy: Mary of Ognies spent thirty-five days in a silent trance, broken now and then by the words, "I desire the body of our Lord Jesus Christ."

The Middle Ages has sometimes been viewed as a time of high-minded churchmen and their powerful authority. In theory, life was regulated by elaborate forms and codes, hedged in by religious rules that had the most awful sanctions. In fact, however, life ran wild, with a defiance of all rules upon which Christians believed salvation depended. Not until the sixteenth century, when organization finally was imposed upon the wide-open university towns, and the Inquisition fell into the hands of an elite, did a sort of terrible order descend upon the Western world: a triumph of righteous aims and powers used toward private aims, and a triumph which, in turn, impelled the mass migrations of minorities to ancient lands newly invaded by Europeans.

This was a frantic era of transition from the classical world to the modern world. Subsequent ages have evaluated the medieval upheaval as both horrendous and sublime. In the late Renaissance and the Age of Enlightenment, writers coined the word "Gothic" to express their contempt for the Middle Ages. The Goths, who were the most effective destroyers of Rome, were looked upon as notorious barbarians. But the Romantic movement reversed this evaluation on discovering the sublime piety of Gothic art. Romantic novels glorified the ideals of chivalry and spiritual love, and recreated a wholly illusionary medieval world. This enthusiasm for the Middle Ages ran its course in the last century, but it left its residue and recently it has been revitalized by the writings of John Gardner and the music of Carl Orff, among others.

The Church offered the Middle Ages a staunch unity of mind, but it failed to lend a unity of lifestyles. A strong regional diversity of customs, which greatly enriched European cultures, was the result of this laxity of Church authority. Today many European patriots look to the Middle Ages for the sources of their national pride. In the breakdown of Roman homogeneity came the birth of individuated cultures and of European nations.

"We have come to the last age of the world," wrote Dante, propelled in his viewpoint by the Faustian spirit, that insatiable, inextinguishable willfulness that distinguishes Western civilization from all others. The power of Rome, which had subjected the lesser regional rulers, and had all but annihilated the concept of the common man, was gone. The restraining influences of the empire gave way to ambitious district rulers and to a resurgence of identity among common people. The very barbarians the Greeks had loathed now found themselves center stage. The Church offered salvation indiscriminately to all, and through holy communion it forgave all sins. To be part of the flock one merely had to come to the Church and abandon heresies. But the old gods were not abandoned. For the peasantry, the echo of fertility magic and fetishes still possessed strong appeal. The Church quickly recognized the force of such prehistoric practices and the more recent influence of such Persian divinities as the sun-god Mithra. To curb the influence of the Mithraic and Cybelic rites, the Christian church permitted the distortion of its own ceremonies by wedding old rituals to new Christian concepts. Thus, the Teutonic rites of the dawn (*Eastre*) became the Christian Easter. A Druid ceremony, with its adoration of trees and the burning of a Yule log, was incorporated into the rites of Christmas — necessitating a decided shift in the date of the birth of Christ.

The accommodational policy of the Church had its limits, however: Roman drama was considered obscene and blasphemous. In fact, all forms of dance and theater were suppressed, at least theoretically. This meant that while the Church of the Middle Ages sponsored music, painting, and architecture, theater and dance were ignored, left in the care of the common people. The Church looked the other way when the commoners flaunted their quasi-ritualistic dances and the nobility welcomed traveling entertainers into their courts. Without Church patronage, dance could only reiterate old forms and did not enter the mainstream of innovative artistic expression which bloomed in the Middle Ages. The brilliant paintings of artists such as Hieronymus Bosch and Pieter Brueghel the Elder depict the exuberance of the dancing of peasants in half-forgotten rites of harvest, marriage, and fertility. But dancing found no patronage, and its social exclusion aided its decline. Acrobatic dances, which probably came from the Orient, became central attractions of song festivals, fairs, and the theatrical pageants. There was a revitalization of ancient dances, whose steps were recalled but whose significance was largely lost. The maypole dance was a focus of fairs and weddings, but its ritual purposes were forgotten. The newly acquired sense of identity among the common people was epitomized in folk pageantry, with its assertive throngs in the marketplace. It was a recovered identity which resounded from a time before the dominance of Rome almost obliterated the tribe's awareness of itself.

In a manner not terribly dissimilar to the strong generational influence of pop culture in the 1960s, the dances of the Middle Ages were an aspect of a politicized culture which provided the masses with a sense of their own priorities, as distinct from the remote and literate powers of the Church. Dance was immediate. Salvation was eventual. In the Middle Ages, the peasantry accepted *each in its own time*.

Henry E. Huntington Library, author's collection

One consequence of this situation was the rise of a nationalistic folk dance related to the emerging nations. Another influence was the Roman pantomimic dance tradition with its affinity for the theater that gradually crept into the depiction of Christian legends performed in churchyards and town squares. These mysteries, miracle plays, and sacred mimes were the antecedents of contemporary theater, opera, and dance.

For a time in the development of dance the symbolism of the Church was balanced against older metaphors. Gradually, however, rites such as animal imitative dances became rare. The hunter culture had become completely replaced by a new agricultural peasant culture. The schism between choral dance, which tended toward dramatic expression, and the dance of couples was indicative of a trend away from imitative and representational choreography, toward abstraction. A common motif in these early national folk dances was the interplay of choral and couple dances, the choral lending a pantomimic suggestion of courtship while the couple dance was abstract, emphasizing the pleasure of movement for its own sake.

The sixteenth century intensified this process toward abstraction, with the development of couple dances consisting entirely of continuous movement of both partners together, as well as those dances in which the partners separated to dance a brief pantomimic episode of flirtation. The pavane, however, was entirely nonpantomimic. The galliard, courante, canaries, and bouffons were still vested with some mimetic images from life. The galliard, after a promenade, called for the separation of the couple and a parade dance of the man in front of his partner in bravuro style. In the courante and canaries, movement expressing coyness and flirtation was performed after the opening, partnered promenade. In the bouffons, procession alternated with chivalrous battle-play.

The second half of the sixteenth century found pantomime in dance so much in decline that the galliard and the courante, and then the canaries and the bouffons, had been restyled as totally abstract, nonpantomimic court dances.

Court dances, the social dances which were performed by nobility, were derived from rustic folk sources. Dancing masters, already prevalent in the seventh century and employed by powerful lords to instruct their courts in the most current dance steps, were maintained in the late sixteenth century by all the great houses of Europe. The dancing master was concerned with more than teaching the art of dance. He was the tutor of the new breed of aristocrats who had only recently emerged from the ranks of petty officials of the expansive Roman Empire. They had ascended by force from the mercenary soldier class or were members of the newly established class of merchants and merchant-princes. There was an effort, particularly in Italian cities where the new nobility lacked prior refinement, to elevate the new elite above peasant manners. It was an era in which rusticity was the most offensive trait in either a man or a woman. The concept of the "gentle-man" and "gentle-woman" became the hallmark of nobility. The dancing master was called upon to prettify folk songs and dances to suit this new world of aristocracy. It was the era which introduced a characteristic Western inclination

The gradual process of dehumanization transformed folk dance into court dance. A Renaissance galliard.

courtesy S. Hurok

The Ballet Folklorico of Mexico, performing a *jarabe* from *The Zacatecans,* recreates folk dance as theater.

Mazowsze, the Polish Song and Dance Company.

courte

ook

In romantic ballets, little remained of folk elements besides costumes, stances, and themes. Mikhail Baryshnikov dances in *La Bayedère.*

that civilization has never lost: the inclination of the "cultured" audience to seek *refinement* rather than *experience* (in ignorance of the fact that the two are compatible and that experience is intrinsic to art). Power and wealth have often been synonymous, but in the era of court dancing, ostentation reached the same sort of excess which may be seen among African chiefs who gorge themselves on food and cover themselves with ornaments as expressions of greatness. In the Europe of courtly dancing, the elaborations of costume reached a point at which dance movement was greatly encumbered. The high steps and brisk turns of folk dancing were necessarily eliminated from court dances. The nobility danced for the sake of social grace and for the exhibition of their finery. Meanwhile, the peasants danced to make themselves happy, to escape the routine of their lives, and to meet their future wives or husbands.

What was once folk dance soon became known as social dancing. Later, in the eighteenth century, the waltz swept Europe. In the nineteenth century, the polka from Central Europe became a favorite; then the Hungarian czardas, the Italian

L. D. Vartoogian

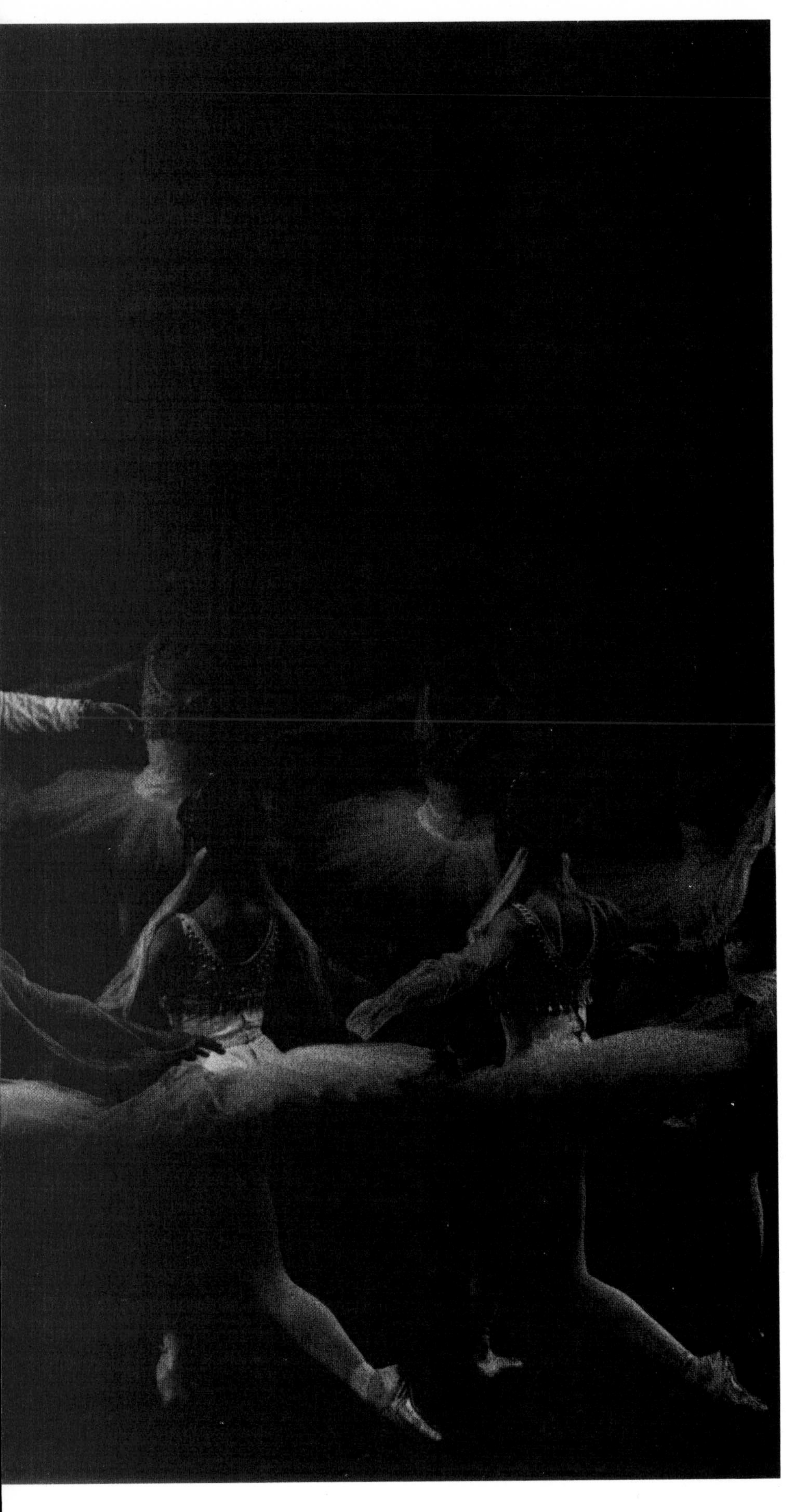

The ultimate image transformed into gods is seen in the Royal Ballet's *La Bayedère*, performed by Monica Mason and Rudolph Nureyev.

L. D. Vartoogian

Ballet abandons fairy tales and reapproaches the contemporary world in Glen Tetley's *Pierrot Lunaire*, performed by Rudolph Nureyev, Johan Eliasen, and Vivi Flindt.

tarantella, the Russian gopak. Social dances tend to travel fast. Early dancing masters discovered methods of notating their dances, and such dance notations were quickly circulated from one royal house to another. Eventually composers were called upon to create special music for the favorite dance forms of the moment, and these compositions also made their rounds of the courts of Europe. This process of borrowing dances from another culture has continued into our own day: for example, the internationalization of regional dances like those of Latin American nations and the dances which have grown out of American jazz and pop music.

Notes on an American Dance Epidemic

Since the turn of the century, America has been the source of most, if not all, new trends in popular culture and, particularly, in popular dance. America was the birthplace of the Charleston in the 1920s, the lindy hop in the 1930s, the jitterbug in the 1940s and 1950s, as well as the dance eccentricities that became

Milton Oleaga

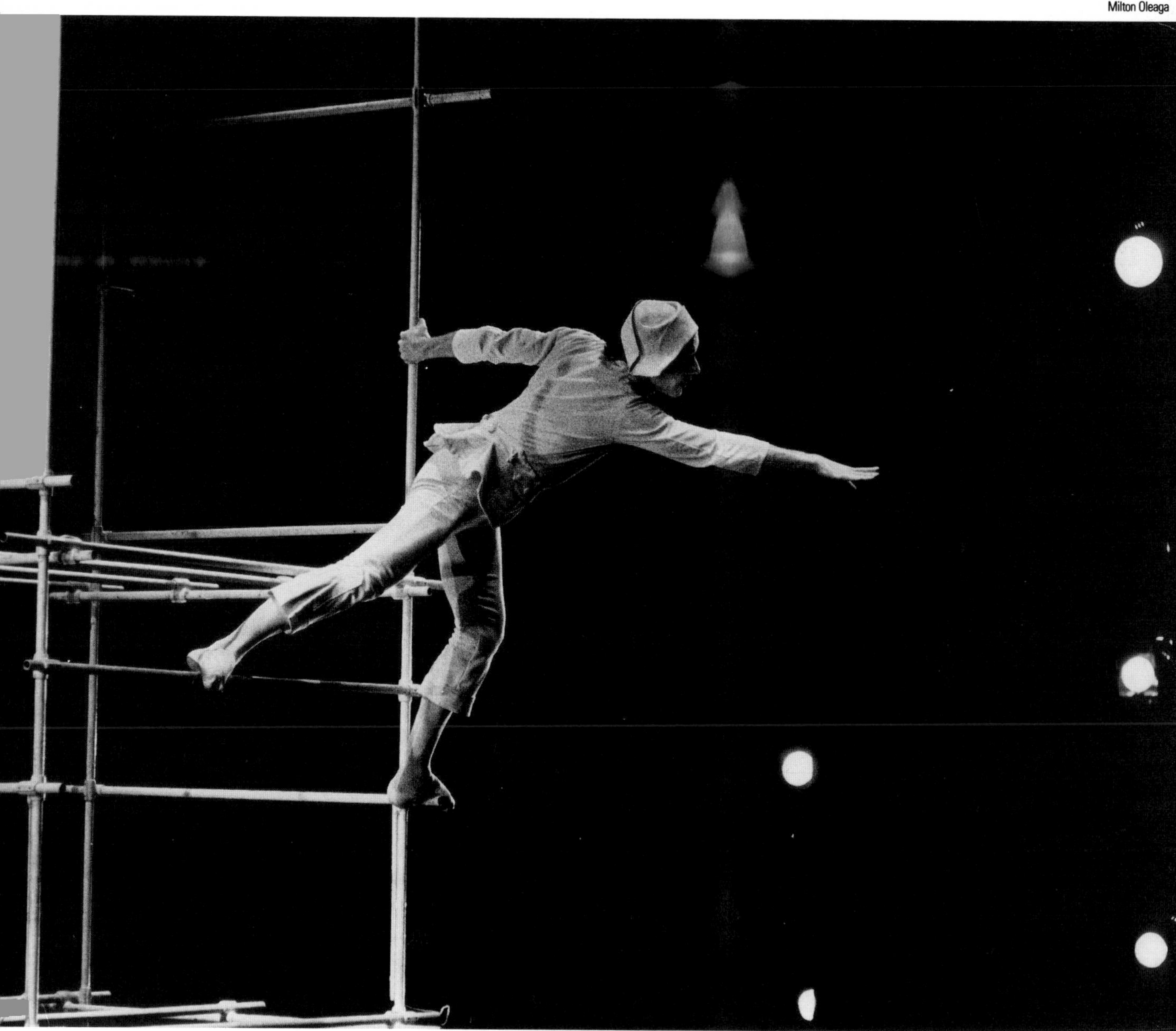

Glen Tetley in *Pierrot Lunaire.*

the hallmark of the 1960s: the twist, hully-gully, bugaloo, stroll, fish, monkey, bug, frug, pony, mashed potato, fly, chicken, jerk, watusi, hitchhiker, freeze, fish, wobble, locomotion, and dozens of other overnight sensations. Then, at the end of the 1960s the rock concert hall took the place of the ballroom and the dancing stopped.

Originally, rock had been a robust, naïve, and admittedly crude music, played by near-amateurs like the Beatles in the early 1960s. Then groups like Cream introduced jazz virtuosity to rock music. Gradually, the era of rock critics and serious listeners began, and people sat down on the huge dance floors where they could listen to the pyrotechnical displays of professional musicians.

Meanwhile, in Europe, the discotheques thrived. In Amsterdam, in Rome, and especially in Paris, fashionably dressed couples trotted elegantly, if rather woodenly, across dance floors in steps that looked like a marriage of the polka and the lindy. The dancing of the 1960s had little influence on Europeans: they never really learned to use their bodies when they danced.

When the rock era ended, it was for some a fortunate return to normalcy. For others, it was the triumph of mediocrity and conformity. Critics announced the decline of political involvement and alternate life styles, which had been ritualized by rock music and dancing. The decline of rock coincided with the rise of the American disco. And the new music, the music of the discos, was not "live," but on discs, played loudly and repeatedly by disc jockeys with a mania for manipulating their audience. The sound satisfied nothing but the feet. The beat was a straight 4/4, without any of the subtle inner rhythms which made rock so sensual and complex and so typical of its era.

There were, however, some reasons to doubt that the world of the discos was as reactionary and mindless as its critics claimed. The disco was possibly the only public place where the major forces of the 1970s rebellion had been totally ritualized into an experience with *real* impact. Social historians often point out that only two motives of the 1960s retained any lasting influence: the sensibilities regarding race and sex. That was where the dance palaces of the 1970s got their essential character. Like the flowering of peasant identity in the folk dances of the Middle Ages, the popular dances of the twentieth century idealized and ritualized the values of a vast new middle class. The complicated social scheme of discos epitomized the sexual and racial ideas of that powerful group. The young disco dancers so completely assimilated novel forms of behavior that they were scarcely aware of doing so.

The dance hall has always been the most conspicuous testing ground for sexual manners — and discos provided a place where new attitudes about sex roles could be freely played out. In the 1970s the idea of couples was so casually treated that single women, for instance, could enjoy themselves in discos without the slightest stigma. Slow dancing to romantic music regained popularity, and the renewed interest in contact dancing brought about a renovation of the lindy and the jitterbug called the hustle, a rather tame dance in which the partners hold hands and pace stridently (with almost no torsal movement) through a succession of solo and duet turns. But none of the new contact dancing put an end to the unique improvisations of the 1960s: people still got up and danced alone or in small groups, and members of the same sex also danced together. Here, in the dancing of men with each other and of women with each other, the disco represented a really major change in convention and sexual attitudes, which affected all dancing, social and theatrical.

Some of the most popular discos in America and Europe were started as gay establishments, which began to open their doors to anyone who wanted to dance. The fact that some discos were gay or "mixed" was casually noted in night-life articles in major newspapers, which took for granted freedoms that until very recently were the basis of scandal.

Although sex has often been noted as the fundamental reality behind the existence of the ballroom, race has not. But there is no question that during the 1960s the attitude of Black people about dancing suddenly and completely reshaped the way white people danced. That sensualization of body movement was absolutely revolutionary, making a significant connection for them between dance, race, and sexuality.

To find a single person who personifies all of these dramatic changes in

American society, we must go back to a white man from Mississippi named Elvis Presley. He learned all that "shocking" dance movement in the South, where people had been "jukin'" for a long time. To "juke" you simply put a nickel in the juke box and let your body loose. Twenty years later, they called the same thing disco.

But all this sensual body motion in the South wasn't merely a matter of doing what comes naturally. Dance is as much as aspect of culture as anything else. Behind everyone who grew up in Mississippi — like it or not — there was a rich Black heritage. So, Elvis knew about the kind of dancing of a dancer named Earl "Snake Hips" Tucker, even though he had probably never heard his name. It was all part of jukin'.

And he knew about Perry Bradford, an old Black man born in Atlanta in 1890. He was part of jukin' too. "Touring the South in them early days," Bradford has explained, "I saw a million steps in a million tonks. The dancers had all kinds of names and no names for them, and I just took over the steps I liked and put them

courtesy of Schomburg Collection, The N.Y. Public Library

Elvis Presley's primitive respectability becomes an American ideal, and suddenly hips go public.

author's collection

in my act. Once in a while, if the step went over big, I'd work up a tune and lyrics that explained how to do it, have it printed, and sell it to the audience after my act."

That is probably the beginning of the whole dance movement which later swept America, and that is how elements of vernacular dance surfaced as sheet music. "The publishers wouldn't take no songs from colored people then," Bradford said, "so I had them printed privately and sold them for a nickel apiece in theaters."

When Elvis emerged from all that unconscious, rich tradition, he was strutting in the shadow of dancers like King Rastus Brown and Bill Robinson, Frank Condos and James Barton, Harland Dixon and John W. Bubbles. If Presley's musical success was beholden to blues singer Arthur "Big Boy" Crudup and to Otis Blackwell, he owed most of his initial fame as a performer to his dancing masters, a whole tribe of black men from minstrel shows and gillies, medicine shows and carnivals, circuses and key clubs, tonks and the Apollo shows. Until the Black choreographic imagination spilled over into white society, the most you could expect at a white people's dance was a polka or a square dance. Even the Irish clog dance wasn't much to rave about until Blacks took it over and turned it into something called tap dancing, which became a whole tradition.

Rock and television grew up together, and Elvis caused the crisis on television which finally broke the boycott of "race music," as the music of Blacks was known in those days. Producers had previously sold a certain amount of Black music and dance in films and on television by "whitewashing" the performers or reducing their acts to Amos and Andy buffoonery. Elvis, however, was a white man (strongly influenced by popular Black culture) and he was a sufficient hit, having sold over 100 million records, to make his meeting with television a commercial inevitability. After one debacle, the cameramen on the next TV show featuring Presley were ordered to photograph him only from the chest up. On Steve Allen's show they managed to dress him up like a pet monkey in formal evening clothes and made him stand absolutely still. The segment was a disaster; nothing happened. "I gotta move," Elvis pleaded. "When I sing I gotta move!"

After three trial-run TV appearances, Presley was finally signed by Ed Sullivan, who patly announced that upon careful review of the performances by Presley on other TV shows, he had not found them too obscene for his own popular family program. Elvis was turned loose and the show's ratings reached an all-time high.

It was never the rockabilly music Presley sang that bothered people. It was the dancing. Elvis was so genuinely hurt by the criticism of his performances and the accusation of obscenity that he once asked his mother if she thought his movements were really obscene. Her reply: " 'Course not, sonny. Trouble with you is that you jest work too hard when you're singin'."

Bo Diddley, the famed Black rocker of the 1950s, remembers that Elvis once asked for his autograph. So Presley may have copied one of Bo's dance tricks—coming out on stage in a crouch while playing a guitar, waving his knees and stamping his feet like a Haitian *rara* dancer. It's more likely, however, that Presley

om the Irish clog dance came an Afro-Amer-n pop dance. Bill Robinson, the first re-wned tap dancer, in action.

courtesy of Schomburg Collection, The N.Y. Public Library

Earl "Snake Hips" Tucker — the return to grass roots, c. 1925.

was an amalgam of many styles. Actually his motions were a relatively tame version of the "Snake Hips" of Black nightclub performers, a dance popularized in Harlem by Earl "Snake Hips" Tucker during the 1920s.

Tucker was the kind of eccentric performer known in the hard-boiled language of show business as a "freak dancer." He came into the New York Black music world of Connie's Inn and the Cotton Club by way of the Maryland tidewaters. "I think he came from one of those primitive lost colonies," Duke Ellington is reported to have said, "where they practiced pagan rituals and their dancing style evolved from religious seizures."

Tucker worked for a short time with Ellington. He wore a loose, white silk blouse with large, puffed sleeves, tight, black pants with bell bottoms, and a sequined girdle with a sparkling buckle in the center from which hung a large, glittery tassel. He had a very disengaged and menacing look, which gave his audience the feeling that he was a cobra and they were mice. He slithered on stage and the audience quieted down at once. Nobody dared to snicker at him no matter how nervous or embarrassed the audience might be. He came slipping and sliding forward with just a hint of hip movement. The step was known in Harlem as "Spanking the Baby," and in a strange but logical way, it established the kinetic theme of his fantastic hip dance. Gradually, as the shiny buckle threw up reflections of light in large circles and the tassel swung into action, the embarrassed audience realized that the dancer's whole torso was becoming increasingly involved in his dance.

The audience, especially the women, were always terribly shocked and impressed by Earl "Snake Hips" Tucker. The message was simple: the tassel was his medium. When Tucker briefly appeared on Broadway in *Blackbirds of 1928*, the press was staggered: "Such coarse suggestiveness should be eliminated!"

The hassle was with the tassel. It was that way in the 1920s for Earl Tucker and it was that way in the 1950s for Elvis Presley. By today, however, not only do we approve of pelvic gyrations, but we have made millionaires of a vast cast of rock superstars who specialize in them. Before and during Presley's initial success, the first major wave of American dances was happening. Line dances performed in groups, such as the madison and the birdland, were the dance hits of the day. By the time the twist made big news in 1960, most young dancers had already abandoned it in favor of a second wave of dances which had evolved out of America's Black heritage, but the frantic dancers were not young people from Harlem — rather, they were the children of middle-class white families. This dance revolution represented a remarkable change in the American idea of dancing.

This wasn't the first time white kids had tried to dance like Blacks. In the 1940s they had painstakingly learned the most acrobatic jitterbug, but their performances were always dull in comparison to the astonishing expressiveness of Black dancers. Behind the white person's inarticulate body were centuries of condemnation of dancing on religious grounds. If the repression of centuries was to be reversed, it would take a momentous hero to make bodily expressivity and intensity attractive to a whole generation. When Elvis Presley made the cavorting of people like Earl "Snake Hips" Tucker attractive rather than offensive to thousands upon thousands of young white Americans, it was a remarkable cultural, sexual, and racial accomplishment. For three or four generations, Americans had been discovering their bodies and the expressive pleasure in using them. The discos of the 1970s were the culmination of that dance impulse which fundamentally altered the American way of thinking about the body, the kind of gestures appropriate to males or to females, to Blacks or whites. It was also doubtlessly a major force behind the so-called dance boom, which sees both theatrical and social dancing as more popular than they have been in any prior decade of this century.

Disco dancing is a mentality, a complex ritual of a specific cultural attitude. It is what pumps life and success into the performances of a sassy dance group led by Twyla Tharp. Disco dancing fabricated a new, cool lifestyle and gave it a place to live. This new cool is made up of equal parts of frenzy, apathy, and fatalism — a bit like the last tango on the good ship *Titanic*. This style became a central theme of many lives in the 1970s. Disco dancing is as clearly a ritual expression of its era as the Dance of Death and the drunken Seven Jumps were of the Middle Ages.

The Ritual Triumph of Death

The fatalistic disco world brings us full circle to the historical point at which we diverged from a discussion of folk dancing in order to chart the development of American pop dancing out of the rustic tradition of the fifteenth and sixteenth centuries. Though popular dance is having a boom on the stage, on the street, and in ballrooms in our decade, it did not fare well under Church authority during the Middle Ages. The influence of medieval dancing diminished drastically as elegant court dance replaced popular idioms. Ecstatic folk dances did not resurface again until the twentieth century, when the middle-class kids rejected polite forms of dancing and invented a renewed folk tradition called "pop."

Dance was originally an ideal medium for the mysticism of Christianity. The Church, however, frowned on dancing partly because of its sexual connotation in the Roman Empire, and also because people still danced to worship pre-Christian gods. But it was impossible to wholly convert people to an entirely new way of life which reflected the theories of the founders and philosophers of Catholicism, so the primal rites of newly converted Christians were reshaped to express Christian doctrine. At first, this religious dancing took place inside the church. A favorite theme for such dances was the imitation of angels' "heavenly rings," a mystic vision of Christian belief which perfectly accommodated the ancient circle dances of pre-Christian rites. "Then shall thou dance in a ring together with the Angels, around Him who is without beginning or end." These words of Clement of Alexandria are reflected in numerous fifteenth century Italian paintings, which depict angels performing a round dance in the fields of heaven, called today by children ring-around-the-rosy. Sacred dances also celebrated anniversaries of martyrs' deaths. The popularity of such dances was at first greeted as an indication of Christian missionary success; eventually, as the Church became more powerful, the emphasis shifted to doctrine, so parables and other educational performances were forced out of the churches and into the cemeteries.

It was in this way that mysteries, miracle plays, and sacred mimes were invented: the dramatization of the delights of salvation and the horrors of damnation, which conveyed moral laws to the peasantry in terms familiar to them in ritual.

Here was a subtle religious revival of the dramatic theater of the Romans which the people loved so much. In their excitement, however, the audience often desecrated the graves, so eventually the Church banned all forms of theatrical presentation. The revival of theatrical entertainment, however, could not be prohibited once it was under way. Minstrels traveled through the provinces, carrying songs, dances, and theatrical shows from one region to another. These archaic entertainers founded the theatrical profession of the Middle Ages and, eventually, the theater of our own day. A medieval joculator had to be several entertainers rolled into one. He sang, he played the harp, he juggled, he tumbled — and, of course, he danced. The tendency to exhibit feats of skill and to indulge in meaningless horseplay was invented as entertainment by these traveling entertainers; and their popular pranks for the peasantry virtually brought an end to any form of expressive rituals in medieval Europe.

Commerce and trade increased in Europe and the towns grew larger. Entertainers formed small troupes, which moved from town to town, arriving in time for a festival day or fair. The wagon-stage, with its flat carriage enclosed on three sides, and the audience seated or milling about in front of the open fourth side, was the "theater" of the day. Despite vigorous Church disdain these troupes drew great

The Coventry Miracle Play being performed on a movable "wagon-stage" in the Medieval age.

crowds and presented acts, mimes, and dances in public squares. Often, the show would close with general revelry and dancing in the streets. Most famous of these troupes of entertainers was the commedia dell'arte of Italy. Built on improvised comedies depicting sexual encounters and homely quarrels, with dancing and juggling fitted between scenes, this interplay of pantomimic drama and folk dance would later influence the form of the ballet.

The nobility often hosted the most renowned of these traveling troupes, but they had also begun their own entertainments in which they themselves often participated as gifted amateurs. The theater created in the great houses of Europe was spectacular. The nobility sponsored these huge spectacles within the great halls of the courts and, as the theatrical plan grew more massive, in the open air. Magnificently decorated floats and costumed courtiers marched in imitation of a Roman general's triumphant parade. At indoor banquets entertainments became fashionable: courtiers danced into the hall carrying great trays of food in a bacchanal spirit. In 1489, for instance, a famous banquet celebrated the marriage of the Duke of Milan to Isabella of Aragon. Dancing servants, disguised as Greek gods, introduced each sumptuous course of the dinner. Floats were drawn into the hall, laden with food and costumed courtiers, whose flamboyant performances were cheered by their peers.

Such spectacles quickly became competitive, one court trying to display greater power and wealth than another. In England, the court masques became opulent. In Italy, the tradition of the genteel masquerade was invented (later to become opera). But these masquerades were entirely divested of the iconography of old dramatic rites in which masked dancers had once represented the powers of nature. The nobility left "nature" as far behind as possible, creating massive headdresses of artificial hair and transforming their bodies into shapes ordained by fashion rather than biology.. The ancient impulse of dance as a kinesthetic rite was lost to a new impulse: the idealization of aristocratic power.

Contrasting with this unyielding demonstration of opulence was the macabre preoccupation of the Middle Ages: the Dance of Death. The old beliefs and the fanaticism of the new Catholic theology — the visions of damnation and the torture of Christ on the cross, the prevalence of pestilence, famine, and warfare — combined into a mystic fatalism unique to the Middle Ages. The Dance of Death, which was never truly a dance, symbolized the essence of the era which created it. The tensions this symbol represented eventually found expression in a psychopathic dance which terrorized much of Europe: the dance mania called St. John's or St. Vitus' dance. This dancing epidemic swept Europe during and immediately after the Black Death. The explanations for this curious form of group behavior include such diverse possibilities as imitative hysteria or a fungus infestation of the rye crops, which resembled the hallucinogen LSD. People danced compulsively, in wild delirium, unable to stop. Often these dances began at funerals and then gathered momentum until they whirled through the streets and beyond the towns, collecting more and more people as they moved along, like the procession of the legendary Pied Piper. In Italy, this malady was called tarantism and was believed to be caused by the bite of the tarantula spider. The Church, in witnessing such demonstrations of seemingly possessed souls, decided that dance was unquestionably a form of witchcraft, and for a time all dancing was strictly forbidden.

The Middle Ages culminated in a philosophy of art which was not to reappear again until the turn of the current century. The medieval idea of art was strongly metaphoric and rarely intellectual. The world of the European peasant was a mystic world not yet bounded by the pragmatism and positivism of the Renaissance. It was a realm of transition in which the creative tumult of nature was still directly experienced and in which the stultifying organization of religion and doctrine was gradually cutting people off from their consciousness of their body.

In the Italy of the Renaissance, the connection between our century and this mysterious medieval world of metaphor was severed. It was the Renaissance dedication to external sensation, objectification, and cool apprehension which gave birth to the ballet.

Ritual into Ceremony

Out of the life of the Middle Ages came many influences ultimately to contribute to the form of a new dance, the ballet. The rich and gorgeous mass of materials found in medieval processions, maskings and mummings, tournaments, and banquet entertainments were so conglomerate and flamboyant that they might never have achieved any semblance of conscious artistry without the particular guidance of Renaissance thinking and the unique sensibility which gave rise to that kind of thinking. The revival of classical scholarship had brought to light the existence of the theater of the ancient Greeks. Though it is traditional to think of Western civilization as a continuous process, in which one era gave rise to the next, as a matter of fact there have been long lapses of continuity. The Church did such a formidable job of obliterating the pre-Christian world that its existence was largely forgotten until the revivalist movement in the Renaissance. The rediscovery of Greek culture with its unity of music, poetry, and dance served to inspire a generation of scholars and artists toward a similar artistic ideal. Their information on the Greeks, however, was meager and largely inaccurate, but a mere glimpse of classical principles was sufficient to arouse a new wave of artistic idealism. In France, shortly after the middle of the sixteenth century, musicians and poets banded together for the purpose of pursuing the revival of Greek concepts of art at the Academy of Music and Poesy, an institution supported by a charter from the king. In Italy, shortly thereafter, a similar group was founded as the Camerata. The French Academy achieved a good deal of stylishness but

Catherine de Médic's 1581 triumph, *Ballet comique de la Reine,* set the style of courtly entertainments.

author's collection

author's collection

Art used to disguise militant muscle, as in this court spectacular, was a politicalization of art.

nothing more, while the Camerata was the basis for the invention of the early form of opera.

This same Greek revivalist spirit was the impulse behind the creation of the first ballet. It came about in the French court, at the instigation of Queen Mother Catherine de Médici. She was the daughter of one of the greatest houses of Italy, where progress in the revival of dance, music, and all the other arts was far ahead of anything the French had yet achieved. When Catherine came to France as the queen of Henry II, she brought with her a company of musicians and dancers. It was their task to supervise the artistic life of her court and to mount unprecedentedly lavish pageants. Catherine wanted to dazzle Europe with her refinement. And that's exactly what she did.

The *Ballet comique de la Reine*, produced in 1581, outdid anything Europe had yet seen in the arts. Catherine, however, was not primarily concerned with artistry. What she was after was political impact, and nothing in her world made a better display of wealth and power than art. This ceremonial sensibility perfectly reflected the era which produced it: garish, aggressive, flamboyant, and vulgar — a vast caste of recently endowed merchants greedy for the plunder of the aristocracy, which in its collapse had opened the flood gates to the avarice of the middle class. One hundred years earlier, the same economic motives had sent land-hungry Europeans to the New World. Now, as the princedoms and city-states vied diabolically for power, those who seized control scrambled to ascend to a position of ultimate sovereignty.

The forces of nature had imbued ritual with its potency. Now, the transformation of ritual into secular ceremonies was impelled by the awe of the political power of man himself. Art perfectly served as the refined guise of an unbounded show of strength. Catherine was without equal, both in her might and in her craftiness. She innovated a method by which she could threaten her peers with muscle cunningly disguised as art. She commissioned the production of "the grandest event of art" to her *valet de chambre*, chief violinist, and dancing master, Balthazar de Beaujoyeulx, who was an Italian despite the Gallic form of his name.

Beaujoyeulx's endeavors on behalf of his queen were enormously successful. *Ballet comique de la Reine* was a dizzy hit, and copies and diagrams of the work were quickly printed and sent to all the courts of Europe. Catherine's political domination was achieved, and the artistic regime of Beaujoyeulx was accomplished. From that time, the French court was the center of the development of ballet. Italy, the original cradle of ballet, now turned with greater interest to opera, which, though it included dance, gave prominence to vocal music. The imagination of Beaujoyeulx was devoted to the opulence of the events he created — spectacles with a strong appeal to the eye. Eventually the resurgence which had given rise to the *Ballet comique* declined, and ballet became a rather insignificant function in the court.

But in the intervening decades before this decline, the delight in ballet performances was enormous. When Louis XIII was king, ballets were presented in front of his City Hall for the benefit of the townspeople. It was Louis XIV, however, who was the greatest royal patron of ballet, and during his reign, ballet reached its height as a form of spectacle, a ceremonial expression of wealth and power, and as a form of artistic creation. In future eras, there would be prestige in commissioning or in owning a work of art, but in the court of Louis XIV the king himself danced. It was a performance not unlike the shaman's ritualistic communion with the supernatural through the power of dancing. But for the shaman, such rites possessed real power which he could tap but not control. Among the courts during the Renaissance and thereafter, nature was subordinated to manicured landscapes and dance was a *device* rather than a *process*.

It is not difficult to see why the sensibility of the Renaissance gave more inportance to the external appearance of dance than to its inner function — or, rather, why the inward satisfaction in dance depended largely upon the perfection of its outward appearance. Today, artists like to use biological terms to describe form in art. These metaphors express the familiar idea that all great works of art must be *organic*. But works of art are not organisms: paintings don't breathe, and sonatas do not undergo life processes any more than poems are capable of propagating. Yet the biological metaphors of art persist. This is probably the case because art achieves the semblance of living form without actually being biological. For instance, a device which creates the sense of movement in art need not actually involve motion. Art is not imitative; it is a projection of human consciousness in metaphoric images. Organic organization is projected into art, but it is not actual. The characteristic unity of life systems, that which holds the whole organism together, is also projected into art. And the methods of fulfilling such functions are different in art from those in an organism, but their apprehensible results are very similar.

Dance, as we have come to think of it, reflects two prominent areas of formal structure: an outer, observed dance and an inner, unseen condition upon which rests the motivational force behind the dance. When these two factors are fused, they achieve the semblance of organic unity.

Sometimes the form of a dance is confused with its structural shape, and its impact is misunderstood as a purely graphic sense of design. The "egocentric space" of dance evolved as a result of secularization and the emergence of social and theatrical dancing. As a nonspectator form, social dances are unconscious of space except as it exists within and between the dancers themselves. The spatial relationship is therefore limited to the positions in space of the partners. In its theatrical form, egocentric space is concerned with the space within the dancer. The dancer wants to demonstrate the finesse of his physical facilities: the height of his leaps, the extent of his extension, the daring of his turns. He does this, however, without any real regard for the totality of space in which he is performing. He is self-absorbed in an egocentric space — his body is the world. Normally, this kind of demonstration of power (and it is indeed a demonstration of physical *power* like the political power exhibited by the patrons who gave rise to this kind of dancing) is offered to an audience from a front-and-center posture in space, simply because this position guarantees the best view of the performer and everything he is doing. A dance, however, has an inner and outer reality: the general outer shape of the dance must be invested with the same interest, inventiveness, and impulse as the inner shape of the dance. It is possible to create a dance which relies entirely upon inward feelings and possesses little external shape. It is also possible to produce a dance which is a pyrotechnical display without any inner impetus or motive. Ideally, dance should be the product of the unity of inner and outer shape — giving it the semblance of organic unity which makes it impressive and significant to the spectator's own biological framework.

In the Renaissance, the instruction of the most famous masters of dance laid emphasis solely upon the necessity of pleasing the eye of the spectator. The dancer was taught to display personal skills and graces. This was the essential nature of the *ballet de cour*, the original form of ballet. Between 1550 and 1700, ballet was largely motivated by class and political ideals which had more concern for fashion than for expressive art. Even today the most difficult revelation to many dance students, who spend so much time thinking about their own bodies and about technical perfection, is the realization of their interaction with other bodies and the greater space they occupy when they dance.

It should not be thought that the *ballet de cour* was entirely devoted to parading voluptuous costumes and displaying technical skills. There remained a largely improvisational creativity for the dancing masters. This period of improvisation in ballet, however, came to an end about 1700 when Louis XIV commissioned Pierre Beauchamp, dance master of His Majesty's Court and *maître de ballet* at the Royal Academy in Paris, to consolidate the numerous steps, postures, and forms of ballet into a limited technical system, reflecting the concept of Copernican order which dominated the Renaissance mind. Such a codification of ballet would bring an end to the unrestrained creative function of dancing masters and would set up a strict mechanistic vocabulary of movement. Thus the *danse d'école* came into existence and the form of dance which is called "classical dance" was founded.

The Ceremonial Mandate

The spirit of the Royal Academy is necessarily authoritarian. Though Cardinal Richelieu did not invent the concept, he was easily the most conspicuous authority of order in his era, and it is not surprising that it was Richelieu who established the French Academy in 1635 — on the eve of the formal emergence of the *danse d'école*, which quickly became the classical dance form we call ballet.

The motto of the French Academy embodied the viewpoint of an age in which rationality became epidemic:

> *To labor with all the care and diligence possible to give exact rules to our language, to render it capable of treating the arts and sciences.*

This was the mentality which dominated the seventeenth century in France and which gave impetus to the codification of ballet.

In the history of royal patrons of the ballet, Louis XIV ranks among the most influential, philanthropic, and, surprisingly, personally gifted as a dancer. When the king's physique grew puffy with middle age he ceased dancing, and the ballet lost its fashionable preeminence at court. This retirement of the dancing king marked a decisive moment in the history of ballet: ballet would either fade away as the craft of disenchanted amateurs or survive by becoming a professional, stable part of the cultural life of the community.

Today, as in the Renaissance, it is the "academy" and other institutions which provide respectability to the arts. This process is essentially one of politicizing culture. It is also a process which persistently preoccupies innovators who urgently need subsidy and often compromise their art for the sake of sociopolitical recognition. In the seventeenth century, it was Jean Baptiste Lully, an Italian-born musician and dancer, who by devious means obtained a charter for a Royal Academy of Music. To that respectable institution he appended the Royal Academy of the Dance.

Of itself, this royal recognition by charter meant very little. But the respectability connected with institutionalization has always been the only means, at least in Western civilization, of making art socially acceptable. Without a charter and the land grant which a charter made possible, the ballet could not have achieved authority in its community. Thus, Lully's next political stroke was to persuade the king to turn over to him the magnificent theater in the Palais Royal, built in 1636 in the Italian fashion a generation earlier by Cardinal Richelieu and more recently occupied by Molière and his company of actors until Molière's death. The Italians had long enjoyed leadership over the French in theatrical innovations and machinery for the production of scenic spectacles and, particularly, in the advance of opera. Richelieu's theater was built with an elevated stage, framed by a proscenium arch, and with the spectators sitting directly in front of the performers — in the style of present-day theaters. The Italians had invested all their interest in opera and had left the development of ballet largely to the French; and in so doing they had steadily conceived of the theater as a more specialized place than the great halls of the courts, where diverse and informal acts and entertainments were presented to gatherings of revelers. The innovations of this new form of stage art spread from Italy to France, fundamentally altering the style of entertainment. The court spectacles had turned entirely from ritual ideals and devoted themselves to cleverness, splendor, and pomp. The new world of the Academy took life more seriously — if not more significantly — and demanded that entertainment turn away from frolic and flamboyance and devote itself to order and clarity. It also became essential for art to be "beautiful."

Among primal people, dance was a ritualistic metaphor of the life process. For the Hellenic world, dance became consciously ceremonialized and was a vehicle for the expression of a humanistic value system. For the princes of the Middle Ages, dance became an entertainment and a vehicle for exhibitionism. With the rise of ballet in the seventeenth century, dance presumed to be "art" and, as such, was expected to possess the contemporary ideals of beauty: clarity and grace.

The greatest technical impact of the new theater on dancing was the proscenium stage. The ancient horseshoe, semicircular design of the seating area was largely abandoned. There is little question that the creation of the familiar turned-out hip of ballet was in part prompted by the frontal orientation of the new theater design. If a dancer chose to raise his leg directly to the front it would appear foreshortened and lack the appearance and clarity of formal design. If, however, the dancer rotated his hip outward and raised his leg to the side, the movement could be seen in profile, while he himself remained facing forward. This motivation probably influenced the universal balletic use of turn-out. The new theater necessitated certain inventions, which gradually gave way to the standardization of a technical code. This systemization was the *danse d'école*, the scholastic dance system we spoke of earlier, which grew out of Lully's Academy of the Dance.

Lully was not alone in his efforts to codify dance steps. Pierre Beauchamp (1636–1705) was the most central figure in this scholastic standardization of ballet. Heading twelve ballet masters at the Academy, Beauchamp codified the gradual unfolding of the mannerisms now typical of classical ballet: the scheme of five positions of the feet, the recognition of the carriage of the arms as standard practice, the naming of specific postures and movements, and the abandoning of others. The very fact that ballet was no longer the entertainment of skilled amateurs, but the work of professionals, stimulated a heightening of technical perfection and a more acrobatic action which appeared daring to spectators who were no longer capable of the dancing they witnessed.

Ever since the linear, mechanistic, and positivist viewpoint of Western civilization was born out of the Renaissance misconception of Greek idealism, people have tried to break loose from their rational bindings at the same time that they have feared anarchy. A major reaction since the founding of the precepts of "the Academy" has been a detested rebelliousness which attempts to loosen those authoritarian commandments that no longer provide a vehicle for the expression of newly evolved values. In philosophy, science, and the arts it became necessary to be a rebel if you hoped to explore new principles rather than rearrange old ones. Dance has largely flourished because of the efforts of such rebels.

The first of the revolutionaries was born after the death of Beauchamp, whose dictates he would revise: Jean Georges Noverre (1727–1810). Influenced by the representational naïve realism of the English actor David Garrick, Noverre was the first choreographer to use the plots of great plays as ballet pretexts. His manifesto, *Lettres sur la danse et sur les ballets*, suggested that steps must be skillful but that skill displayed for its own sake was unaesthetic. Dancers, he stated, should make steps and gestures which reveal the feelings of the

represent. Noverre rejected as inartistic the kind of ballet which only wanted to impress with flamboyant technique.

Marie Sallé, before Noverre, had also concerned herself with the expressional purposes of dance and criticized technique which was incapable of supporting feelings. She wanted to abandon the set costume of ballet and to dress each character in something that approached naturalistic appearance. The directors of the Academy violently opposed Sallé's ideas. She was forced to leave France and go to London where she presented her ballet, *Pygmalion*, in which Galatea wore Greek draperies instead of the conventional *panniers* and jeweled headdresses of the *danse d'école*. Sallé's reforms however left room for more rebellion — she wore the Greek-inspired draperies over the conventional corset and petticoat. And it was not until Noverre that a thorough revision of ballet began. Like the concepts of Sallé, Noverre's ideas were rejected by the directors of the Royal Academy of Music and Dance. The influence, however, of *Lettres sur la danse et sur les ballets* gradually crept into the sacrosanct institution by way of the young dancers who greatly admired Noverre and were intrigued by his philosophies. Slowly, the use of the techniques of the antiquated mask were abandoned; costuming was reformed to a certain extent, and the new principles of verisimilitude made themselves felt in subtle ways. These new values, along with the advocacy of plot and purpose as the basis of ballet, were facets of what Noverre called "the ballet of action."

Whereas ballet had previously existed as a tangent of musical entertainment and the vehicle for virtuoso performers, it now became the medium of theatrical action and plot. By 1770, the once independent and nationalistic arts of French ballet and Italian opera had been fused, standardized, and highly rejuvenated by Noverre's ideals. Eventually, another rebellion would take place (in our own century) when Michel Fokine would demand a revision of ballet not unlike that of Noverre's.

The ballet of the Academy was ideally suited to the age which produced it. There have been many subsequent rebels who have used the stultified *danse d'école* as a target for their criticism, but they have sometimes accused ballet of an inertness and formalism which was abandoned generations ago. Since Noverre shook the foundations of the authority of the *danse d'école* it has been under persistent revision — as malleable an art form as any other. The history of ballet's evolution, decline, and rejuvenation reflects countless values of the societies in which it was prominent.

In 1650, the ballerina was unknown. Boys danced all female roles. But by 1850, so great was the interest in the newly installed ballerinas that male ballet dancers had become rare. Subsequently, the male was subordinated to a position of partner, lifter, and poseur. Women, who began so unimportantly in dance, eventually asserted more power in the theater and, especially, in dance than in probably any other profession until recently. Their emergence in the theater was very gradual. They first appeared in the ballet *Le triomphe de l'amour* in 1681. Their success on stage was enormous, although it in no way constituted any semblance of the social prestige afforded male dancers in the prior era. On the contrary, the female's stage appearance was scandalous. Despite the low rank which automatically fell upon any woman who danced professionally, many skilled women began dancing. Soon the rivalry between prima ballerinas was notorious. Marie Sallé, known for her dramatic prowess, and Marie Camargo, illustrious as a technician, were dread enemies. The ballerinas soon eclipsed the dancing masters, the choreographers, even the authority of the Academy. Their impact on a large and powerful public was so great they were able to assert an influence previously unavailable to commoners. Much of the subsequent evolution of dancing as an art and as an increasingly expressive form was the achievement of exceptional female dancers and choreographers.

Other factors also influenced dance. The pseudo-Hellenic revival was over. The romantic era swept Europe, bringing to a close the rule of the Academy and the strict rational mentality it represented. With the era of romantic rebellion came the ideals of the common man, individualism, full-blown sentiment, and the evaluation of intuition as superior to rationalism. For centuries, males had prided themselves upon their special facility for intellectual authority. They had, meanwhile, attributed to women the very "faults" which the romantic movement now idealized. This view of women became central to the arts.

The romantic movement also revived an admiration for an era which the Age of Reason had despised: the Middle Ages, with its mystic dualism, which saw man torn between the spirit and the flesh. The folklore of the Middle Ages — with an emphasis upon a totally idealized vision of peasant life — also became a central theme of the new spirit of romanticism. Supernatural creatures fell in love with mortals who came to inescapable, tragic ends. The ephemeral and spiritual always triumphed over the mortal. The soft focus (so conspicuous in later impressionism) took hold in the romantic age, and the lines between dream and reality, mortals and immortals, were blurred and prompted the recovery of some of the metaphoric implications of preclassic ritual forms.

In ballet these new principles had an impact so great that all but the superstructure of the *danse d'école* was reshaped to suit the artistic malleability of the new sensibility. This era produced two of the earliest ballets still performed in the repertory of international companies: *La Sylphide* and *Giselle*. And these were the ballets that gave additional impetus to the reign of the famous ballerinas of the romantic period.

Maria Taglioni gained fame as *La Sylphide*, a frail heroine from the spirit world. Taglioni was the idol among the dancers who characterized spirits, while Fanny Elssler was famous for her earthy heroines. La Camargo was the first ballerina to raise her skirt several inches and to remove her heels. Shorter skirts eventually led to the mid-calf tutu which we know today in ballets like *Swan Lake* and *Giselle*. Flat shoes led to slippers with blocked toes for dancing *en pointes*, a technique very well suited to the spiritual creatures the romantic ballerinas portrayed. Male dancers also danced *en pointe*, however the interest in the female dancer had by this date so subordinated the male that women "*en travesti*" now took the roles of men and frequently women danced both male and female roles in *pas de deux* which depicted love scenes.

The golden era of ballet took place in the 1830s and 1840s, with ballets created by Jules Perrot, Charles Didelot, Auguste Bournonville, Filippo Taglioni, Jean Coralli, Arthur St. Leon, and Paul Taglioni. Of these, only *La Sylphide* and

author's collection

The rise of the female in the arts, of which Maria Taglioni in *Flora et Zéphire,* 1830, is an example, introduced a new sensibility at the same time that it sexualized art.

Giselle remain extant. This golden era saw the power of the prima ballerina rise to such a level that audiences (not unlike the new audiences for ballet in the 1970s) paid little attention to the choreographer's art. They came to see the technical feats of the stars and little else intrigued or impressed them. The prima ballerinas were so indulgent that they accepted this glorification without realizing that it was part of the deterioration of their art. Ballets gradually became showpieces with little or no value as choreographic art. Any development of dance forms or dramatic forms which did not center on the prima ballerina was discarded in favor of pyrotechnical tricks suited to the conspicuous skills of a particular dancer. By 1870 ballet began to decline: every aspect was as theatrically formulated as it had been rationally formulated during the era of the Academy. The plots were standardized, and the climax of the performance was always the *grand pas de deux* by the bejeweled prima ballerina and her dutiful cavalier. This set-dance was constructed in a standard four-part form consisting of a duet called the *adagio,* followed by a solo or variation by the man, a solo or variation by the woman, and a final *coda* in which the two partners danced together again, using very rapid and brilliant steps rather than the sustained postures of the opening

The oldest surviving ballets of the popular repertory. Karen Kain and Frank Augustyn in the National Ballet of Canada's *La Sylphide*.

Natalia Makarova and Mikhail Baryshnikov in the American Ballet Theatre's *Giselle*, 1975.

adagio. Many of the ballets of this era have survived in popular repertory in the much abbreviated form of *grand pas de deux*.

Curiously, this touting to public taste brought about the financial ruin rather than the success of ballet. Audience interest shifted from the showcases of ballerinas to the musical theater where humbler forms of dance offered even easier amusement.

Revolution in the Academy

A famous late nineteenth-century cartoon, *Apocalypse du ballet*, depicts dancers as whirling tops and as acrobatic legs topped by smiling faces. From the standpoint of cultural history this humorous view of ballet accurately summed up both its artistic status and the general disinterest of the public. Ballet was no longer the court favorite and its vitality suffered from many of the same maladies which produced the decline of the aristocracy that created and sponsored it. From its inception, the *danse d'école* was wholly concerned with the pleasures of a dilettante audience and its peculiarities of taste. The degeneration of ballet was the result of prolonged superficiality in the choreographic art itself, as well as the rise of a popular mentality which liked elegance less than it liked acrobatics. The music hall audience certainly had a dim view of ballet, but the decline of dancing was caused by more than banal tastes in entertainment. Ballet itself permitted an excess of social pretensions and it indulged the whims of its most famous exponents. The age of great ballerinas ended in an egocentric star system, which made more of privilege than artistic skill. The audience and the stars insisted upon the repetition of the same acrobatic combinations, even when such pyrotechnics were entirely unsuited to the theme of a particular ballet. Consequently, the imagination which had originally forged the most important aspects of ballet very nearly vanished. By the end of the nineteenth century "choreographers" were little more than dutiful orchestrators of the tasteless whims and ostentations of ballerinas. In France, where ballet had originally created a triumph, it was dismissed as passé. But in Russia, where classical dance had arrived late, ballet was reaching a stage of lavish decadence.

The supreme power behind Russian ballet was French-born Marius Petipa, who reigned at the St. Petersburg Imperial Theater. Petipa's achievements were less impressive for their choreographic skill than for the brilliant music he employed in his ballets. Before Peter Ilich Tchaikovsky began to compose formal dance music for Petipa, ballet was generally considered unworthy of serious composers. The best that could be expected was mediocre music like that of Ludwig Minkus. The premieres of Tchaikovsky's ballets went far in altering that dogma. *Swan Lake* improved the regard for the marriage of ballet and music when it was premiered in Moscow in 1877. It was probably the first ballet score to use leitmotifs to depict characters and situations. This technique provided the steps with a cohesion and impact which they might not have otherwise possessed. The second act of *Swan Lake* (by Lev Ivanov) has survived as the most popular of romantic ballets, but by many standards that wasn't good enough. Acts I and II of *Swan Lake* (by Marius Petipa) were products of a superficial, pantomimic dance idiom totally out of touch with the aspirations of the other arts of the time. Despite moments of musical and choreographic magic the arch-conservatism of the Academy stifled his creative imagination. The rigid beauty, the absolute symmetrical forms, the ideals of clarity and precision, even the total remove from a new mentality which was shaping the late nineteenth century provided Tchaikovsky's ballets with an impact similar to the monumental decorative style of painter Puvis de Chavannes — particularly his *Life of St. Genevieve* series in the Paris Pantheon. His carefully arranged compositions were far from profound but were, for the time, eminently acceptable.

By 1890, when *Sleeping Beauty* was premiered, ballet consisted of five positions of the feet, five positions of the arms, five positions of the head, about 100 miming gestures, seven basic movements *(plier, entendre, relever, glisser, sauter, élancer, and tourner)*, and about fifty steps of which *pirouette, entrechat, tour en l'air, arabesque*, and *attitude* were the most easily recognized by an audience of ballet enthusiasts. A sequence of these movements and positions made up an *enchaînement*. Linked *enchaînements* formed a variation. Variations for the leading dancers and the movements of the *corps de ballet* made up the whole performance.

Such a strict framework was bound to rouse rebelliousness. This rebellion, like the political struggle of the new proletariat of the era, was built upon the effort to overthrow an obsolescent Russian aristocracy. In dance the revolutionary heroes were two exceptionally willful and talented artists: the Russian, Michel Fokine, and the American woman from San Francisco, Isadora Duncan.

The Russian school of decorative realism thrives in the international repertory with wedding cakes that tell stories. Here the New York City Ballet performs *Nutcracker*.

Martha Swope

courtesy of S. Hurok

Rudolf Nureyev and Karen Kain perform in the National Ballet of Canada's *Swan Lake*.

To understand the basis of their dance revolution we have to back up a bit and take another look at the events in ballet which preceded the turn of the century. While dance was rapidly growing into a French and Italian tradition, the rest of the world had largely retired from any emphasis upon the choreographic art. All the forms of ritual and folk dances persisted in Latin America, Oceania, Africa, and in many parts of Europe. This preclassic tradition was the rich reservoir of the new dance forms which were about to emerge. It was in the spontaneous vigor of folk dance, the uncorseted sensuality of peasant ritual, and the sentimentalized concept of Greek idealism that Isadora Duncan found a basis for her rustic American dance. Fokine, however, did not abandon ballet as Duncan did. The product of a robust Russian classical tradition, he insisted upon preserving it even though he battled its formalism.

Fokine's reverent basis for continuing the lineage of ballet came from countless Slavic outposts where ballet had flourished since the days of Peter the Great. Peter was a man of considerable enlightenment and vision, inclined to favor internationalism rather than strict Russian nationalism. He admired the achievement of the West and opened the doors of his country to many Western influences. His example changed the future of Russia. In 1738, the Empress Anna created the Academy which persists to this day under the patronage of the Russian government. Catherine the Great sustained the concern for ballet, inviting French and Italian experts to her court and producing a flamboyant international style, which laid stress upon French aristocratic pretensions.

The arty world of Catherine the Great had little room for the rustic heritage of Russia. It took the audacity of a 24-year-old graduate of the Academy to express the dissidence which was creating progressive and conservative factions in every department of Russian life. Michel Fokine addressed his scholastic superiors with a series of criticisms of the strictness of the Academy ideologies. Like Noverre before him, his complaints were presented in the form of a letter which repeated many of Noverre's earlier demands for a revision of the *danse d'école*. Fokine, however, was the product of 125 more years of balletic evolution than Noverre, and his platform was highly innovative — consisting of five major points which were strikingly similar to the ideals later endorsed by Isadora Duncan and the ensuing generations of modern dancers.

Fokine insisted that classroom techniques be abandoned and that every ballet should have a style of movement suitable to the nation and the period in which it was laid; that the action of a ballet should be continuous instead of being divided by pantomimic sequences and pyrotechnical displays for self-serving soloists whom

Maya Plisetskaya performs in the Bolshoi Ballet's *The Dying Swan.*

L. D. Vartoogian

he abhorred; that the archaic mime of opera-ballet be discontinued and that the dramatic action of the dance be served by the entire body of the dancer at all times rather than being confined to the rigid use of the arms and legs without the inclusion of the torso; that not just the soloist but the entire company of dancers be employed to evolve the dramatic theme and to be expressive rather than keeping the *corps de ballet* for purely decorative interludes; that music should no longer be a mere succession of little dance tunes but should possess a unity which carries the dramatic intent of the dance forward; while scenery and costumes should possess the greatness of art and not a flamboyant and erroneous imitation of the decorum of a past age. For instance, Fokine bitterly condemned the use of *pointes* in ballets concerned with ancient Greece, on the basis that such slippers were anachronisms and that bare feet would be more appropriate.

That Fokine's concepts seem to us today to have been devoted to a naïve realism is unimportant. Whatever his motives, the result of his criticism broke down the academic conservatism of ballet and introduced ideas which would eventually alter the entire basis for creating dances — whether balletic or modern.

As one might expect, Fokine's concepts were angrily rejected by the Academy. For Fokine the rejection was painful, but it was a fate which he shared with a whole generation of innovators: Duncan in dance, Debussy in music, Cézanne

J. L. Vartoogian

A scene from the ballet — Cynthia Gregory and Ted Kivitt in the American Ballet Theatre's production of *Grand Pas Classique*.

in painting, and Frank Lloyd Wright in architecture. Fokine's was an era of enormous upheaval in which the new was battling the old, but no art form was as out of step with its age as was the balletic world of fables and fairies envisioned by Marius Petipa.

Like many rebels, Fokine was silenced by being sent off by the Academy to "a distant outpost," along with several other young eccentrics. This peculiar troupe of young Russians was headed by a flamboyant visionary of the theater named Sergei Diaghilev. Diaghilev, who had been associated with the Academy in an administrative capacity, requested to arrange a tour of certain rebels during the long summer vacation. The Academy was more than happy to be momentarily rid of the argumentative young students and artists. They had no idea that the appearance of this newly formed Ballet Russe would cause a sensation, ushering in a golden age of ballet.

The concepts of Michel Fokine were popular among the rebels of the Ballet Russe troupe. As for Diaghilev, he possessed a keen ability to unite the talents of various young artists and to fire their efforts with daring and high style. In its day the Ballet Russe was seen as the realization of the ultimate unification of the arts. Today we are inclined to see the Diaghilev company as a highbrow circus which did not represent a complete amalgamation of the arts but, instead, a conglom-

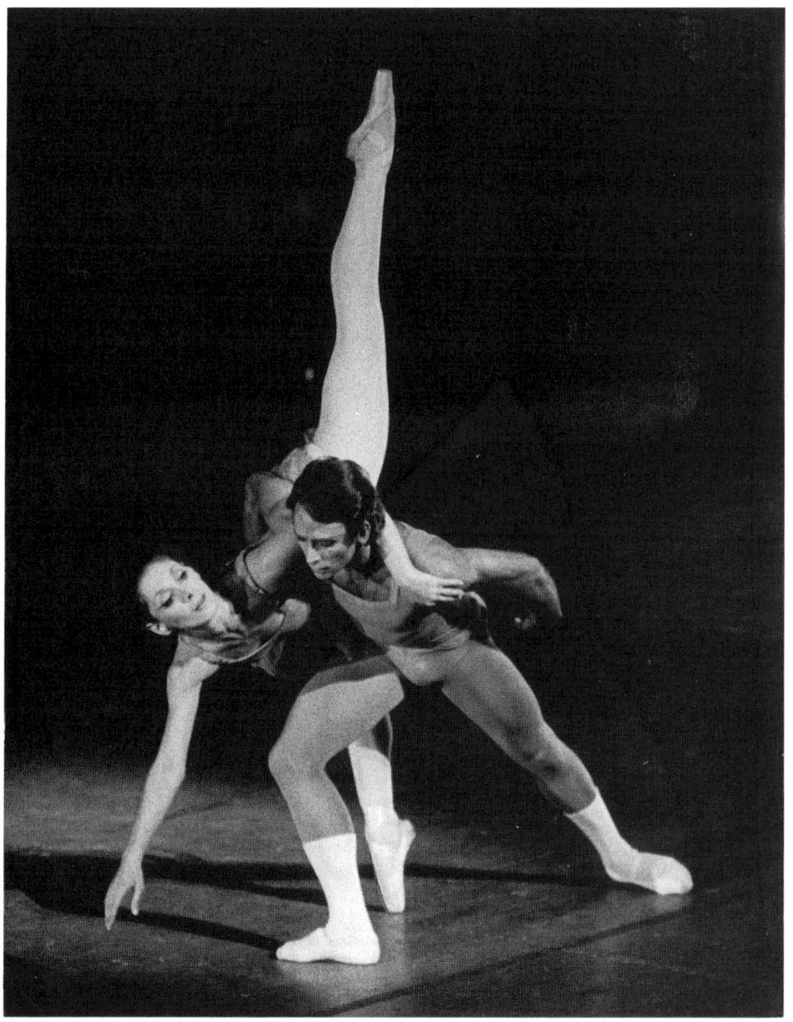

Martha Swope

Cynthia Gregory and Ivan Nagy dance in the American Ballet Theatre's production of Kenneth MacMillan's *Concerto*.

Martha Swope

Natalia Makarova and Fernando Bujones in the American Ballet Theatre's *Le Corsaire.*

eration: vast imaginative paintings used as backdrops but not constituting a real innovation in scenic art; utterly intrusive costumes designed by painters who had little or no comprehension of the potential of bodily movement; the use of magnificently original music which, in its advanced aesthetic ideas, was far too advanced for the choreographic forms which even the most liberated of the Ballet Russe choreographers contributed. Despite such criticism there is no question that the Ballet Russe provided important innovations, while it also surrounded itself with sufficient excellence in the related arts to establish a prestige for dance hitherto unobtained. There were also several great artists of the company: among them Anna Pavlova, Vaslav Nijinsky, and Sergei Lifar. Nonetheless the creative imagination and daring works created by Fokine for the Ballet Russe were childlike by comparison to the creations of the other artists associated with Diaghilev: Stravinsky, Picasso, Debussy, Ravel, etc.

Many of these collaborators — and Stravinsky in particular — were impelled by one of the most important motives of twentieth-century art — to rediscover through entirely contemporary idioms the authentic basis of primal (and often nationalistic) ritual forms. In the *commedia dell'arte* influences of his *L'Histoire du soldat* Stravinsky reached into the Middle Ages for an inspired theatrical

cia Haydee and Richard Cragun in the
gard Ballet's *Romeo and Juliet.*

all photographs author's collection

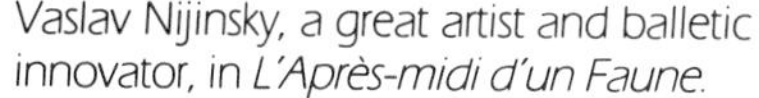
Vaslav Nijinsky, a great artist and balletic innovator, in *L'Après-midi d'un Faune.*

Vaslav Nijinsky in Michel Fokine's *Petrouchka.*

Vaslav Nijinsky as the favorite slave in *Schéhérazade.*

example. And in his creative folklore — like the peasant opera-ballet *Les Noces* — and his ferociously primal evocation of Russia's prehistory, *Le Sacre du printemps*, Stravinsky introduced ideas which brought music into a new expressive era.

By comparison, we must admit that the balletic concepts of Fokine were rather timid — especially if we compare his Arabian "ritual" called *Schéhérazade* to Stravinsky's evocation of Russian folk rites in *Les Noces*. It is interesting that Nijinsky, aspiring to choreograph his own works, seems to have outranked Fokine for sheer inventiveness. When he choreographed Debussy's *L'Apres-midi d'un Faune* he completely departed from the balletic principles of the Academy because he felt that traditional steps and postures could not cope with the vision of the highly original score. And in 1913, when Nijinsky choreographed *Le Sacre du printemps*, he used entirely unorthodox movement, which was every bit as responsible for the ensuing riot at the premiere as the music of Stravinsky.

Whatever the artistic shortcomings of the Ballet Russe, it is clear that the company was an essential testing ground for rebellious, often brilliant collaborators and was the crucible for an era of innovation. In associating with the greatest artists of his day Diaghilev was able to produce a more important moment of ballet history than had existed for any prior age. With Poulenc, Auric, Milhaud; Satie, de Falla, Laurencin, Picasso, Derain, Pruna, Rouault, Stravinsky, Benois, and Bakst as collaborators, it is little wonder that the fame of the ballet company of Imperial Russia became so great that it eclipsed all other efforts — even the works of Marius Petipa. The impact of the Ballet Russe was so great that there was a long period when dancers simply had to adopt Russian names if they were to be

fabulous partnership — Anna Pavlova and Vaslav Nijinsky in *Pavillion,* 1907.

L. D. Vartoogian

L. D. Vartoog

taken seriously. The Ballet Russe dancers so dominated the attention of the dance audience that for two generations the emergence of an American ballet idiom was effectively delayed. The founding of a valid idiom of ballet in the United States might have been even more delayed had it not been for the originality of an Americanized Ballet Russe alumnus named Georgi Melitonovitch Balanchivadze — known today as George Balanchine.

What that young man from St. Petersburg — together with several generations of American choreographers — created in the name of ballet is so basically removed from the *danse d'école* that it is unrealistic to call it ballet. This is not to dismiss ballet but to place it realistically in history. The beauty of ballet is undeniable. Even if we qualify our admiration by suggesting that our enjoyment is conditioned by centuries of expecting dance to look like ballet, we still must recognize the aesthetic virtues of this graceful idiom of dance, whose formal attitudes have, reasonably or otherwise, provided a basis for most dance techniques in the West. At the same time we must ask some questions of ballet. For instance, what actual impact did Noverre have on ballet? Do the repertory's oldest ballets — *Giselle* and *La Sylphide* — maintain a tradition comparable to the great musical and literary works contemporary with them?

Giselle was premiered in 1841, a time which also saw the introduction of the works of Karl Marx, Charles Darwin, and Herbert Spencer. It was the decade of the music of Chopin, the *Faust* of Goethe and the *War and Peace* of Tolstoy. The modern novels of Balzac (who didn't die until 1850) were being read on the day that the whimsical fairytale *Giselle* was premiered. Dostoyevsky was engaged in a stark psychological realism in his novels, while Browning was inventing the interior monologue in poetry. And Richard Wagner (who was almost 30 when *Giselle* was premiered) was reshaping the entire notion of the musical theater. What then is *Giselle* all about? Why is it commonplace for such staunch balletomanes as England's Arnold Haskell to admit the artistic slightness of *Giselle* and at the same time to state that "it stands alone in fulfilling the conditions laid down by Noverre"?

And what do we say about the second great rebel of ballet — Michel Fokine? Why do critics readily admit that his ballets are rather dated, faded by forgetfulness, lost under the dust of late Victorianism? Why is *Schéhérazade* so embarrassing? Why does *The Fire Bird* seem so undistinguished by comparison to its magically inventive score by Igor Stravinsky? What finally is *Petrouchka* but a splendid pantomimic vehicle for three brilliant actor-dancers?

These questions became the basis of a dominant consensus of the state of dancing. Debates which have not yet concluded divided the public — a faction adoring the very qualities which another faction saw as weaknesses. For the first time a serious literature of dance began to be written and critics with perspectives in art history began to be heard. They asked if ballet might have been better off without Noverre and Fokine. It seemed to many critics of ballet that just what Fokine and Noverre found deficient in ballet was inherent in its origins. Noverre called for a return to Greek ideals, but ballet was founded upon an erroneous

argot Fonteyn and Rudolf Nureyev in Frederick Ashton's *Amazon Forest,* 1975.

aya Plisetskaya and Alexander Godunov in the Bolshoi Ballet's
rformance of Roland Petit's *La Rose Malade,* 1973.

The many faces of ballet — Birgit Keil of the Eliot Feld Ballet Company in Feld's *Impromptu.*

Susan Miller and George Montalbano of the Eliot Feld Ballet Company in Feld's *Intermezzo.*

concept of classical Greece which persisted despite the subsequent clarifications of historians: at the end of the nineteenth century the Kirov Leningrad Ballet Company — which was the original producing group of Petipa — continued to dress the Greek gods and goddesses of the final act of *Sleeping Beauty* in the costumes of Renaissance courtiers. Both Noverre and Fokine sought a realism of which the ballet was incapable; a realism it could achieve only by the use of the old-fashioned pantomime both Fokine and Noverre detested. Court dance and the ballet of the Academy were abstract forms intent upon the attractiveness of movement itself. No one imagined dance to be the serious art which we insist it is today. And no one thought the worse of dance for being ephemeral and built upon a technique which was not very capable of supporting expressive content. Many defenders of ballet pointed out that their apppreciation of the old idiom is no more or less significant that the admiration of a large public for Louis XIV antiques. They also point out that those who make new ballets built on strict classical techniques are doing something no different from the architects who still produce major civic and private buildings created on Romanesque designs.

Through the prominent examples of Isadora Duncan, Loie Fuller, and Mary Wigman the autonomy of the Academy was finally broken, and a fundamental revision in the concepts of what dancing is and what it can be has occupied choreographers and critics ever since. This era of speculation gave birth to modern

Susan Cook

Johan Elbers

Christine Sarry and Mikhail Baryshnikov in Eliot Feld's *America*.

The American Ballet Theatre performs Mikhail Baryshnikov's *Nutcracker* in 1977 with Baryshnikov and Marianna Tcherkassky dancing.

dance. It also provided the basis for a renewed energy and imagination in ballet. Unwilling to abandon classical dance but prepared to redefine all but its most basic ideals and techniques, a succession of choreographers established new virtues in ballet: Kurt Joos, Antony Tudor, Agnes de Mille, Eugene Loring, and Kenneth MacMillan created some of the most influential dances. Jerome Robbins produced ballets of a completely eclectic idiom, as much derived from modern dance, personal invention, primal and jazz dance as from classical ballet.

A central influence in the revision of balletic ideas was the emergence of an American dance idiom. The artists of the United States had usually regarded their folk tradition as hopelessly inferior to the grand heritage of Europe. This attitude, however, underwent a drastic change, and by the 1940s American genre works were among the most interesting signs that ballet could deal with people and places other than those familiar in fairytales. In Philadelphia, Catherine Littlefield was attracted to the kind of dance impulse which had animated the rustic folk dances of preclassical times, and she created American "folk" dances for her company. In New York, in the 1930s, Lincoln Kirstein was an outspoken defender of ballet against the onslaught of new trends. He sponsored experiments in ballet which gave rise to such talents as the young Lew Christensen, who made a ballet called *Filling Station*. Eugene Loring, Kirstein's most impressive discovery, produced *Billy the Kid*, which became the first cowboy classic of American ballet.

The marriage of contemporary sensibility, political protest, and modern art. Kurt Joos in *The Green Table*, 1977, performed by the José Limón Company.

Johan Elbers

L. D. Vartoogian

In Jerome Robbins' *Fancy Free*, danced by Buddy Balough in this American Ballet Theatre performance, America enters ballet with overtones of vernacular dancing and the cult of youth.

Agnes de Mille created *Rodeo* — an ideal blend of ballet and cabaret dancing and realistic pantomime. The jazz ballet *Fancy Free* by Jerome Robbins with a score by a young composer named Leonard Bernstein was unquestionably the triumph of American genre ballets — catching the spirit of the times, depicting familiar, contemporary characters, and shaping these elements into a dance idiom equally indebted to Beauchamp's codified ballet and the musical extravaganzas of Hollywood films.

Jerome Robbins turned the focus of ballet on the theater. As a result his dances became highly theatrical. They also became progressively ritualistic — a process visible in his fascinating ballet *The Cage*, his reworking of *Afternoon of a Faun*, and his dance entitled *Watermill*. Such ritualistic sensibility was entirely new to ballet, an ancient impulse of dancing which the Renaissance dancers had steadfastly ignored in their longings for the "high" civilization of Greece rather than the powers of primal peoples. As the consciousness of ritual forms became

courtesy PBS

The American mythos in dance is seen in Eugene Loring's *Billy the Kid*, performed by the American Ballet Theatre's Marianna Tcherkassky and Terry Orr.

In every American there is a lonesome cowboy — the American Ballet Theatre performs Agnes de Mille's *Rodeo*.

Milton Oleaga

In Jerome Robbins' *Afternoon of a Faun,* performed by the New York City Ballet's Allega Kent and Francisco Moncion, Robbins turns his rich theatrical imagination from Americana to "things without words."

Martha Swope

The New York City Ballet performs Jerome Robbins' *The Concert.*

The New York City Ballet performs *The Cage* by Jerome Robbins.

Martha Swope

Martha Swope

Edward Villella in the New York City Ballet's production of Jerome Robbin's *Watermill.*

Mar

The New York City Ballet performs Jerome Robbins' *Ballets: U.S.A.*

The era of psychology dawns in ballet — Gelsey Kirkland and Erik Bruhn in the American Ballet Theatre's performance of Antony Tudor's *Jardin aux Lilas.*

J. L. Vartoogian

apparent to choreographers — especially those devoted to modern dance — the way in which they imparted dramatic content in their works began to change. The realistic aspects of plot, chronology, and characterization as well as causal relationships were either abandoned or submitted to a drastic ritual process. Unlike the old ballets which attempted through the use of pantomime to transform realistic literature into comprehensible dumbshows, young balletic choreographers like Jerome Robbins and the British-born Antony Tudor reconstituted their subject matter into elements unique to ritual action. They did not "stage a story" or put together pleasant dance steps into little staged numbers; instead they produced moving images with metaphoric powers to deeply move their audiences. This special process of distillation and ritualization was later borrowed by the dramatic theater. For instance, Clive Barnes in *The New York Times* observed that Robert Montgomery's stage adaptation of Dostoyevsky's *The Idiot* was so radical in idiom as to require the playwright to subtitle it "A *response to Dostoyevsky's The Idiot*." Barnes clearly saw that what Montgomery had done with the Dostoyevsky novel was similar to the way in which Martha Graham approached Greek myth. Montgomery stated: "*Subject to Fits* is absolutely unfaithful to the novel; it uses the novel for its own purposes; it does not hold the novel responsible. As such, it is entirely original — smacking of *The Idiot*, dreaming of *The Idiot*, but mostly, taking off from where *The Idiot* drove it."

Antony Tudor and Jerome Robbins taught ballet how to dream, how to take off from its subject matter. It is unquestionable that they learned to fly by watching the early exponents of modern dance, who rejected ballet entirely and sought an alternative basis of dance.

Not all the choreographers of ballet wanted to fly, however; some were determined to keep one foot in the nineteenth century so they could uphold the

L. D. Vartoog

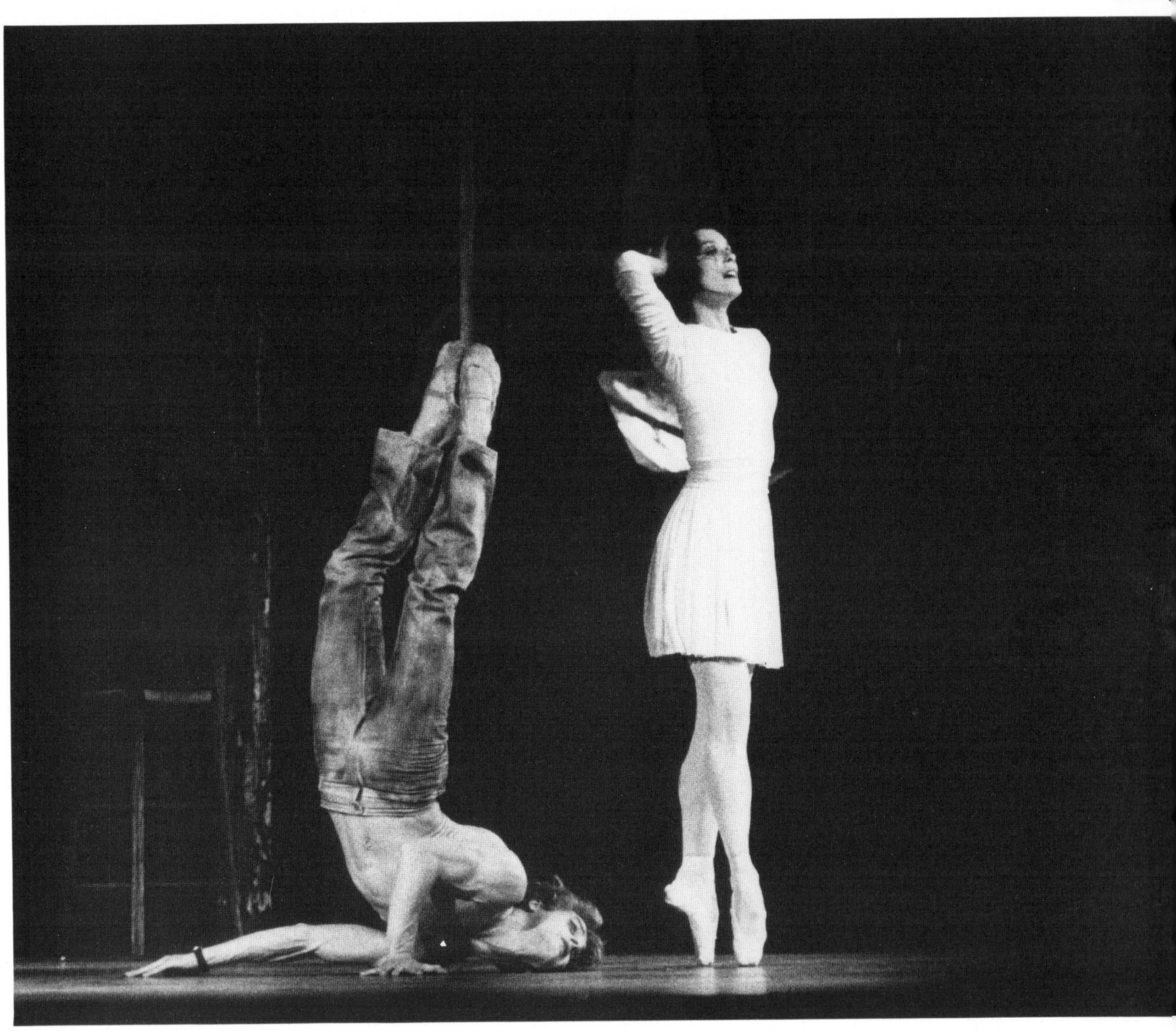

Mikhail Baryshnikov and Bonnie Mathis dance Roland Petit's *Le Jeune Homme et la Mort,* which is based on a pretext of Jean Cocteau and optimizes the surrealistic mentality.

classical ballet tradition. George Balanchine is the most accomplished of such traditionalists. He frankly considers himself the heir to Petipa's legacy at the same time that he has produced brilliant balletic mutations in response to the challenge of the music of Igor Stravinsky, a composer with whom he often collaborated.

Lincoln Kirstein went to Paris in 1933 to invite Balanchine to America. The gifted, young choreographer accepted on the condition that he would have both a dance company and a dance school. At the School of American Ballet, Balanchine wisely trained his future ballerinas from childhood. He clearly saw the potentialities of the unique physique of the American girl: long legs and sturdy frame quite unlike the women of Europe. He admired a "kind of angelic unconcern toward emotion as a special charm of the American dancer." He noted that they do not wear emotions on their sleeves like the grand divas of the Petipa and Diaghilev eras; they manifest whatever feelings they have directly in the drama of the dancing body itself. This American manner concurred with Balanchine's disposition for pure balletic form without narrative plot. His interest was essentially in dances without stories, in which movement was self-explanatory and self-sufficient. In this way, Balanchine ritualized his balletic mentality; he rejected psychological narratives and pantomimic storytelling, and he also rejected the mindless and expressionless spectacles which had dominated ballet at the end of the nineteenth century. He was essentially more revolutionary than Noverre or Fokine. He was not interested in the "ballet of action" of Noverre or the balletic realism of Fokine; and he wasn't attracted to the nonchalant, pyrotechnical displays which prima ballerinas had made famous at the expense of balletic art in the nineteenth century. To the contrary, Balanchine subordinated the ballerina to the intent of the choreography — and his ruthless methods of dealing with willful dancers became renowned. What he wanted and what he found he could achieve with the unique abilities and cooperative spirit of American dancers was an idiom of ballet in which expressiveness is intrinsic to movement. An ideal exemplification of these ideals is found in *Serenade*, surely one of the most enduring dance works. It is an eloquent ritual, unique in its perfect expression of a contemporary attitude toward classical balletic ideals. No one knows precisely what *Serenade* "means," but everyone who has seen it is certain that it possesses a

Mikhail Baryshnikov in Roland Petit's *Le Jeune Homme et la Mort.*

L. D. Vartoogian

curious, ineffable significance as art. It is the kind of significance which only becomes visible in dance.

For many choreographers, however, Balanchine's genius reveals only a small part of the greater world which dance is capable of envisioning. These people believe in an entirely different and alternative dance idiom. And so they turned away from both Balanchine and ballet and went in search of a future in art which revived the most important essence of the past which had been lost in the avalanches of time and progress.

The Return to Ritual

In 1905, a Rubensian woman named Isadora Duncan danced throughout Imperial Russia in order to "show that classical ballet was all wrong." She believed that dance should not be the repetition of ready-made steps. It should be free. It should express the feelings and ideas of sensual people rather than depict fairy tales. It should forget its stuffy traditions and roam freely where it would, barefooted for the sake of control and also in order to display the beauty of the human foot, naked or near-naked to extol the human body. And transparent in its feelings.

Some of these rebellious notions were not entirely new to the Russians, for Michel Fokine had argued in behalf of a liberated dance form. The difference between Fokine and Duncan was her determination to leave ballet entirely to the age that created it, just as Cézanne, Frank Lloyd Wright, and Debussy left Rembrandt, Chalgrin, and Wagner in order to discover unique ideals applicable to their own age. Here, however, Fokine hedged — he wanted to sustain balletic tradition, in the belief that it was a classical aesthetic form and not simply the projection of a bygone era. Yet Fokine was highly attracted to the flamboyant Isadora and her radical ideas about dancing.

This fascination and friction between modern dancers, who follow the Duncan example, and ballet masters, who uphold Fokine's unfailing belief in ballet, widened during the next twenty-five years. Curiously, the debate has diminished in recent times to such an extent that the differences between modern and balletic ideas are less dramatic than they were when Isadora sailed off for Russia.

There are two important bases for Duncan's divergence from the dogma of ballet. The most significant and ultimately the most influential for both modern dancers and ballet choreographers was her rejection of ballet as a ceremonious and decorative activity. Instead, Duncan envisioned dance as a personal ritual capable of supporting both ideas and feelings. Ballet was clearly a corporate form, built upon decades of codification and standardization. This was a major reason why Duncan rejected it. She believed that the validity of ballet had vanished along with the validity of the aristocratic and corporate mentality which had produced it. She was a child of a new era of individualism. What she sought in place of balletic conformity was a dance which glorified the self. In other words, she envisioned a personal ritual.

The second important basis of Duncan's divergence from balletic dogma was her *physiological* comprehension of dancing — a viewpoint that rejected the tendency in ballet to use the dancer's body merely as an implement to produce pleasant external shapes. Duncan was concerned with the inner, kinetic motivation of dancing, the *motor intelligence* that provided the dancer with an articulate body. She envisioned motion as an activity which commenced in the solar plexus and then undulated muscularly into the rest of the body. Duncan's inclination to talk about "the science of movement" was entirely new — something Noverre and Fokine had apparently not considered in their own criticisms of and attempts to reform ballet tradition. Duncan wanted to start from scratch, to ask questions which balletic tradition precluded.

She gradually evolved a theory of the physiology of dance, insisting that movement and breathing are inseparable, that all movement is carried aloft and returned to the earth (the center of gravity) by inhalation and exhalation. Duncan also recognized that bodily motion stimulates empathy in the onlooker's body. As dance critic John Martin stated: "These principles are at least as old as man himself; primitive societies have found them so potent that they have called dance magical and based religious and social practice upon it. But these principles had never been consciously utilized as the basis of art until the turn of the present

In every American, there is a vulnerable woman. A parody of vulnerability and ballet's grand manner is the target of Trocadero de Monte Carlo's *Les Biches,* 1976.

Johan Elbers

century when Isadora Duncan made them the very center and source of her practices and the so-called modern dance was born."

An associate of German choreographer Kurt Joos was so impressed by Duncan's ideas that she permanently abandoned the Joos Ballet Company and took up a lifelong exploration of modern dance. Her name was Mary Wigman and, along with Isadora Duncan, she gave substance to the wholly new idiom of dance which has dominated this century and which is one of the few generic arts produced in America. Also important as forerunners of modern dance was the American theatrical dancer Loie Fuller and the team of Ruth St. Denis and Ted Shawn, whose exotic productions suggested to a worldwide public that there were dance idioms besides ballet which deserved the designation of "art." It was from the school of the illustrious American couple — Denishawn — that Martha Graham, Charles Weidman, and Doris Humphrey emerged to become the Holy Trinity of dance in the United States and the first true exponents of a revolutionary form which has been called modern dance, expressionistic dance, contemporary dance, and — by its detractors — barefoot ballet.

Through the efforts of this brilliant triad of choreographers — along with several generations of their followers — modern dance has taken a general shape

Lois Greenfield

The Time before the Time after (after the Time before), performed by the Lar Lubovitch Dance Company's Susan Weber and Aaron Osborne, stretches the limits of the balletic mind.

courtesy German Information Center

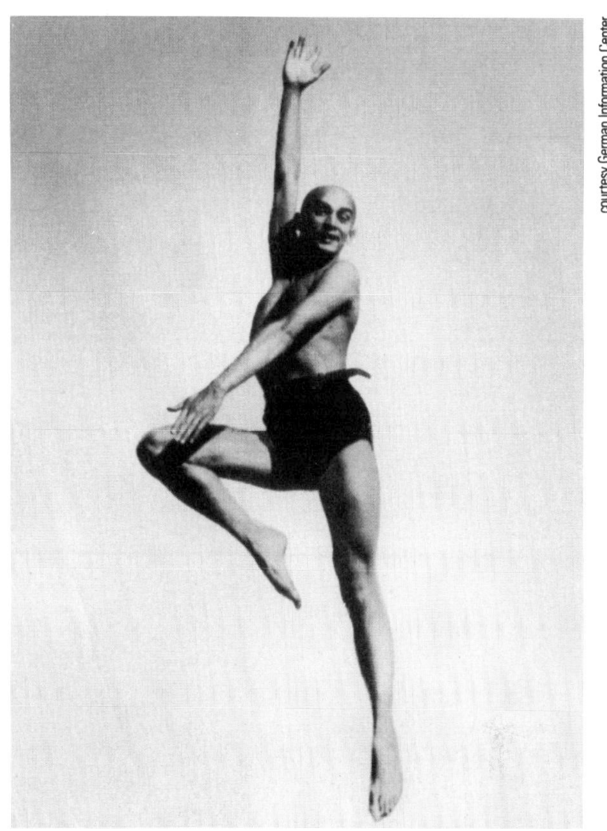

courtesy German Information Center

The German connection — Mary Wigman and Harald Kreuztberg relive life through dance rituals.

and form. The name "modern dance" is inept, for there is nothing modern about modern dance. It is essentially the most basic, the oldest form of dance despite its reputation as an avant-garde idiom. "The modern dancer, instead of employing the cumulative resources of the academic tradition (*la danse d'école*) cuts through directly to the source of all dancing," wrote John Martin during his days at *The New York Times* when he was the primary apologist for the new dance idiom.

Much early work in modern dance was self-exploratory, the search for a pure dance concept without undue dependency upon musical accompaniment, the quest for nonmimetic gestures which were expressive without being representational, and the founding of a basis for the collaboration between composers and choreographers which would produce a new relationship between movement and music. But the most imperative research among the pioneers — which continues as the basis for a succession of rebels — was concerned with the discovery of the physiological, emotional, and aesthetic principles that govern movements of the body, their range and limitations, as well as the constant redefining of what is and is not proper in a dance and what, "artistically" speaking, dance is fundamentally all about. Thus, in a very real sense, dance in this century has remained primarily a personal ritual operating, like most avant-garde art, as an idiosyncratic form rather than a tribal expression of religious powers or a corporate expression of societal values.

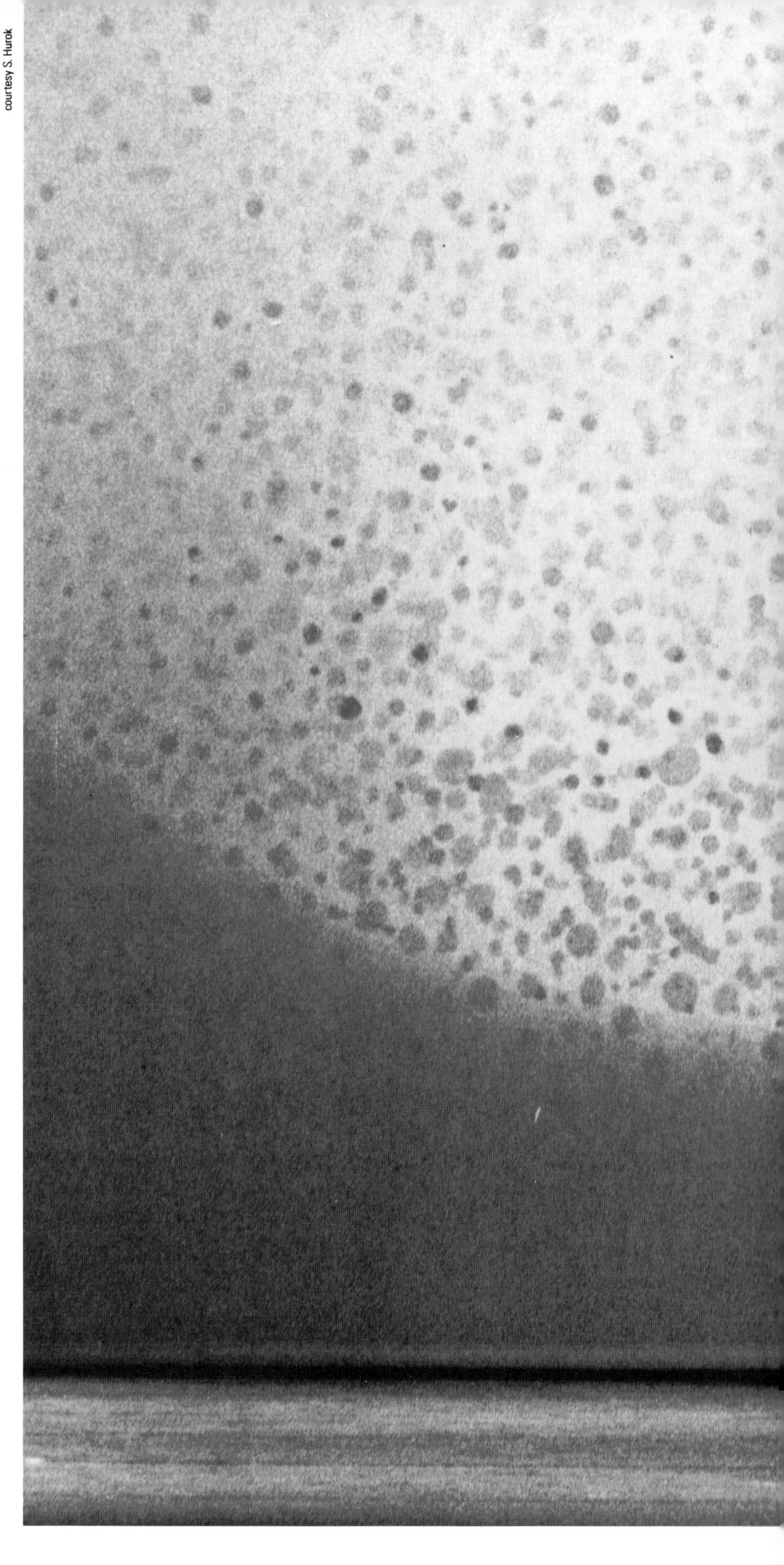

courtesy S. Hurok

Glen Tetley has keenly and uniquely merged the expressiveness of modern dance with the techniques and structures of ballet. Here the Stuttgart Ballet performs Tetley's *Voluntaries*.

Idiosyncratic Ritual

Though composer John Cage is unquestionably a vital and dominant power behind idiosyncratic art in our era, he is sometimes more visible than substantial. Clearly, he is the most articulate American art philosopher of our era ("We must begin from scratch!"), but many forces, not just one, are behind the avalanche of activity that produced the art idioms that are fundamentally an "avant-garde for the masses." The pop sensibility of people like Andy Warhol, Claes Oldenburg, and Roy Lichtenstein; conceptual art and minimalism; the triumph of pop music and its special mentality; and the aesthetic implications of the music and ideas first of Anton Webern and then of Karlheinz Stockhausen have all produced a wave of exploration which questions most of the dogma of prior art.

Johan Elbers

Maurice Béjart invented an avant-garde for the masses: a new theater filled with popular symbols and personal passions. Here Béjart dances in his company's performance of *Faust*.

What is art? What is suitable for a work of art? What is the commonplace and why must it be included or excluded from art? What is noise as related to sound and to music, and why is it necessarily excluded from the works of composers? What is the role of the artist and how much control does he or she really have over what is produced? What is skill and what is technique and why are they necessarily imperative in a work of art? Why must art be beautiful and how can we define beauty?

The experimental urge is largely an American phenomenon, and it reflects the undercurrents and impulses of the gigantic energy and productivity of the United States in the years since World War II, when individuality in conflict with conformity evolved a unique American mentality which we cannot yet wholly understand, though it is reflected everywhere in American art and society. This trend made its first impact in the experimental films of the 1940s which took a drastically revised view of experience, reality, and, along the way, morality and aesthetics. Many of these filmmakers were dancers, and even those who weren't — Maya Deren, Willard Maas, Kenneth Anger, Curtis Harrington, Gregory Markopoulos, and Shirley Clarke — nonetheless used dance as a matrix in their work. The new art mentality became prominently visible in painting as well as theater and poetry. Ultimately all of these media merged in ritualistic events called "happenings." From such multimedia theater pieces emerged three important artists: composer John Cage, painter Robert Rauschenberg, and choreographer Merce Cunningham — one of the first to break away from representational, expressionistic dancing and to reject self-expression as a central purpose of dance.

Jamake Highwater

Béjart's Ballet of the 20th Century performs *Petrarch: The Triumph of Time.*

Coming out of this revisionist view of art (though each possesses a unique impetus and purpose) is a succession of exceedingly unorthodox and often brilliant choreographers: James Waring, Ann Halprin, Twyla Tharp, Gus Solomons, Jr., Yvonne Rainer, Rudy Perez, Meredith Monk, Viola Farber, James Cunningham, Lucinda Childs, Laura Dean, Wendy Perron, Trisha Brown, Judith Dunn, and Nancy Meehan, as well as many others. Certain general aims could be seen in the works of many of these innovators. There was a highly rarified — if not always consistent — inclination to espouse the antipersonality viewpoint of T.S. Eliot, who said: "The poet has not a 'personality' to express, but a particular medium, which is only a medium and not a personality." Curiously the result of this aesthetic, when applied to dance by some choreographers, has been a basis of self-expression which verges upon primal scream.

Another preoccupation of many choreographers has been the ideas of Rudolf Arnheim, who is clearly not impelled by naïve realism in his own insightful writings on art but who has nonetheless induced a good deal of naïveté among those who read his words: "The dancer does not act upon the world, but behaves in it." Taken together with the example of minimalists and conceptualists, Arnheim's statement might be a good summary of the ideals behind the works of the Judson Dance Theater in New York, where Yvonne Rainer, among others, was a key figure. The Judson Theater became specially known for dances which revolved around the performance of ordinary actions in relationship to ordinary

Jorge Dunn and Victor Ullate in Maurice Béjart's *Nijinsky, Clown of God.*

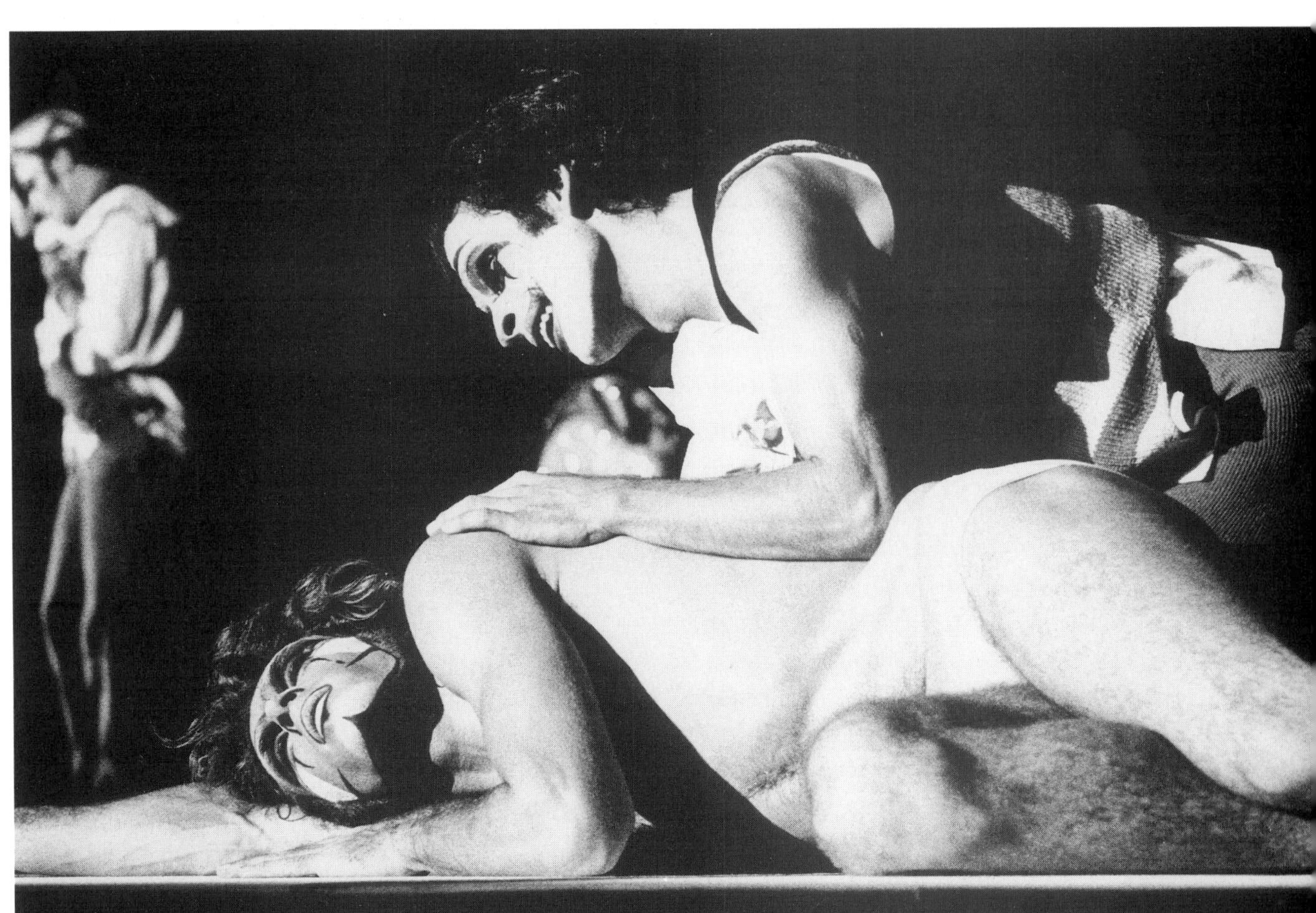

J. L. Vartoo

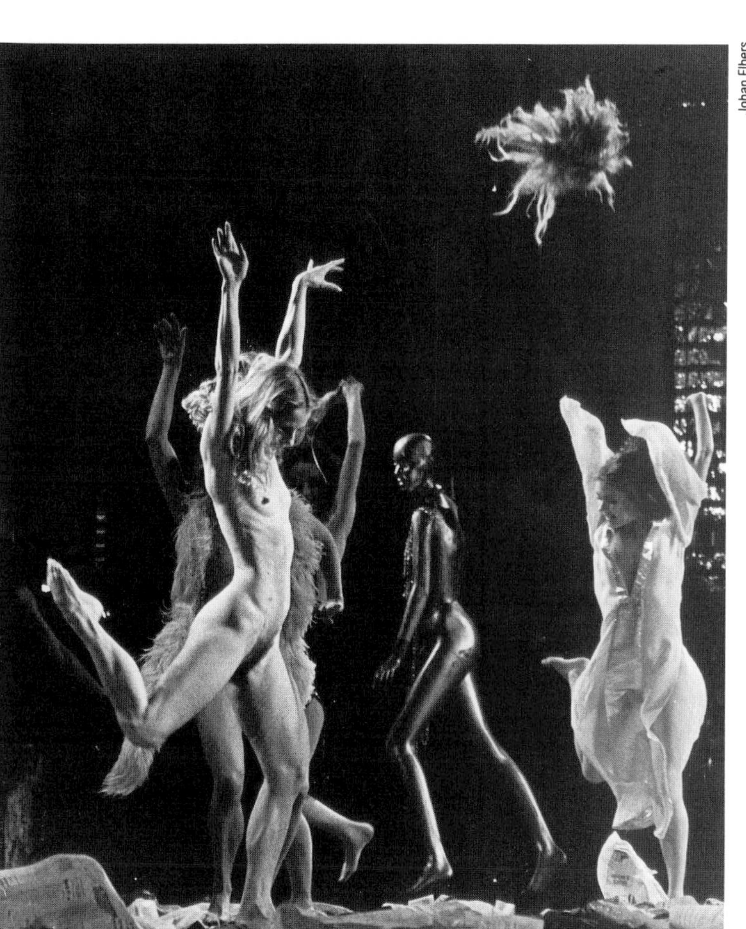
Johan Elbers

Triumph of Death, performed by the Royal Danish Ballet, is in the idiom of Maurice Béjart, but with a Danish difference.

objects. These dances were devoted to a matter-of-fact, concrete, and banal reality which clearly redefined dance as "anything which happens." Or as the late James Waring once said: "Dance is any aimless movement — any movement without an object in mind. . . . Art is anything you point your finger at and say, 'This is Art.' "

Dance critic Marcia B. Siegel touches upon the motive for these trends: "An inevitable reaction against the highly individual aesthetics of the modern dance matriarchs (Graham, Humphrey, etc.) set in as soon as their followers began to choreograph. The present generation of dancers seems to be primarily under the influence of three men, all of whom have deliberately turned away from the introspective, cerebral, moral concerns of the early moderns. Erick Hawkins emphasizes the sensual, Alwin Nikolais the pictorial, and Merce Cunningham the kinetic possibilities of movement." Siegel is a strong advocate of the cosmos of Cunningham: "Dance is what you want it to be, no one can interpret or structure another's dance for him; dance is of the moment and any form of analysis or reproduction destroys it. Today's young dancers seem to have a deeper conviction than ever before that a literal approach to dance is a bad approach."

Dance critic Walter Sorel is not equally devoted to the Cunningham school, but he admires Cunningham himself: "If there is such a thing as a meaningful world without conventional meaning, he creates such a world. He denies that he

J. L. Vartoogian

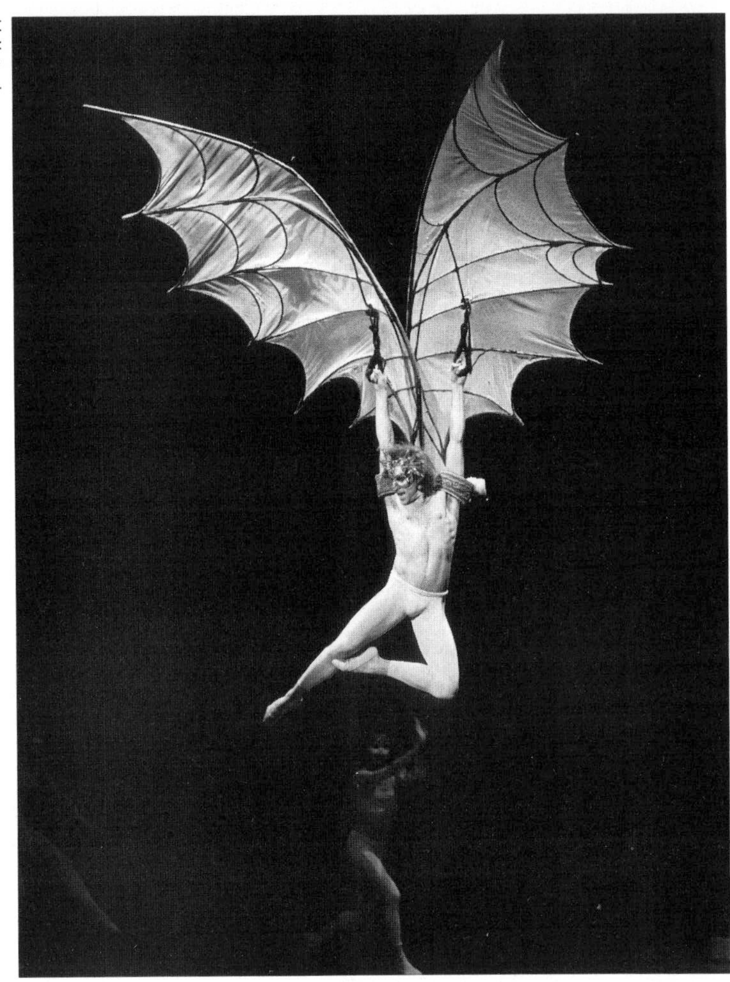

Jorge Dunn as Icarus in Maurice Béjart's *Faust.*

wants to say anything, and certainly he constantly uses surprising images and the most unrelated forms. Despite the lack of emotional unfolding, his dance creations are specific in their moods—lyrical, satirical, or pensive. However detached they try to be, this dance remains a triumph of humanness, full of the warmth of an eternal emotion."

Cunningham, however, is not alone, Erick Hawkins and Alwin Nikolais are also exceptionally important influences among young dancers. Nikolais comes to dance by way of the theater and his work requires us to completely redefine what we mean by dancing, since his performers rarely *dance* in the accepted sense of the term. Nikolais produces a theatrical totality which has as its dramatic impulse a uniquely magical and atmospheric vision of technology. Even in his fundamental concept of motion, as sublimely exemplified in the dancing of Murray Louis, Nikolais uses mechanism as a curiously poetic force, suggesting, but never actually imitating, the well-oiled moving parts of a miraculous apparatus. Yet this movement idiom is capable of the most intense feeling without the slightest intrusion of emotion; as, for instance, in the brilliant male-female duet which, for me, is the centerpiece of Nikolais' most important work, *Imago.*

Nikolais is not drawn to psychological theater. He envisions quite a different cosmos—one in which beings halfway between mechanisms and persons undertake movement that depicts a world of microbes and asteroids—things beyond the reach of the naked eye. This kinetic world is created by Nikolais himself—he produces the electronic scores, the astonishing costumes, as well as the imaginative lighting effects which ushered in the era of light shows long before such a pop term existed. The result is total theater in which narrative content is rejected in favor of an experience produced by depersonalized bodies moving through an environment with the expressiveness of a metaphoric language of the future.

Erick Hawkins builds his concept of dance upon a vision of "the body as a clear place." His entire focus is on the body as the only source from which dancing can originate, and as such his theory is exceedingly sensual and exclusively concerned with *exactly* what happens when human beings move. His first principle seems to be a response to the old preconceptions of dance movement: "The error consists in believing that because it is possible it is desirable." He sees a link between the current reappraisal of uncontrolled childbirth, the concentration of wealth, and

Ceremonies in a new imagery.—the Alwin Nikolais Dance Company in *Grotto*.

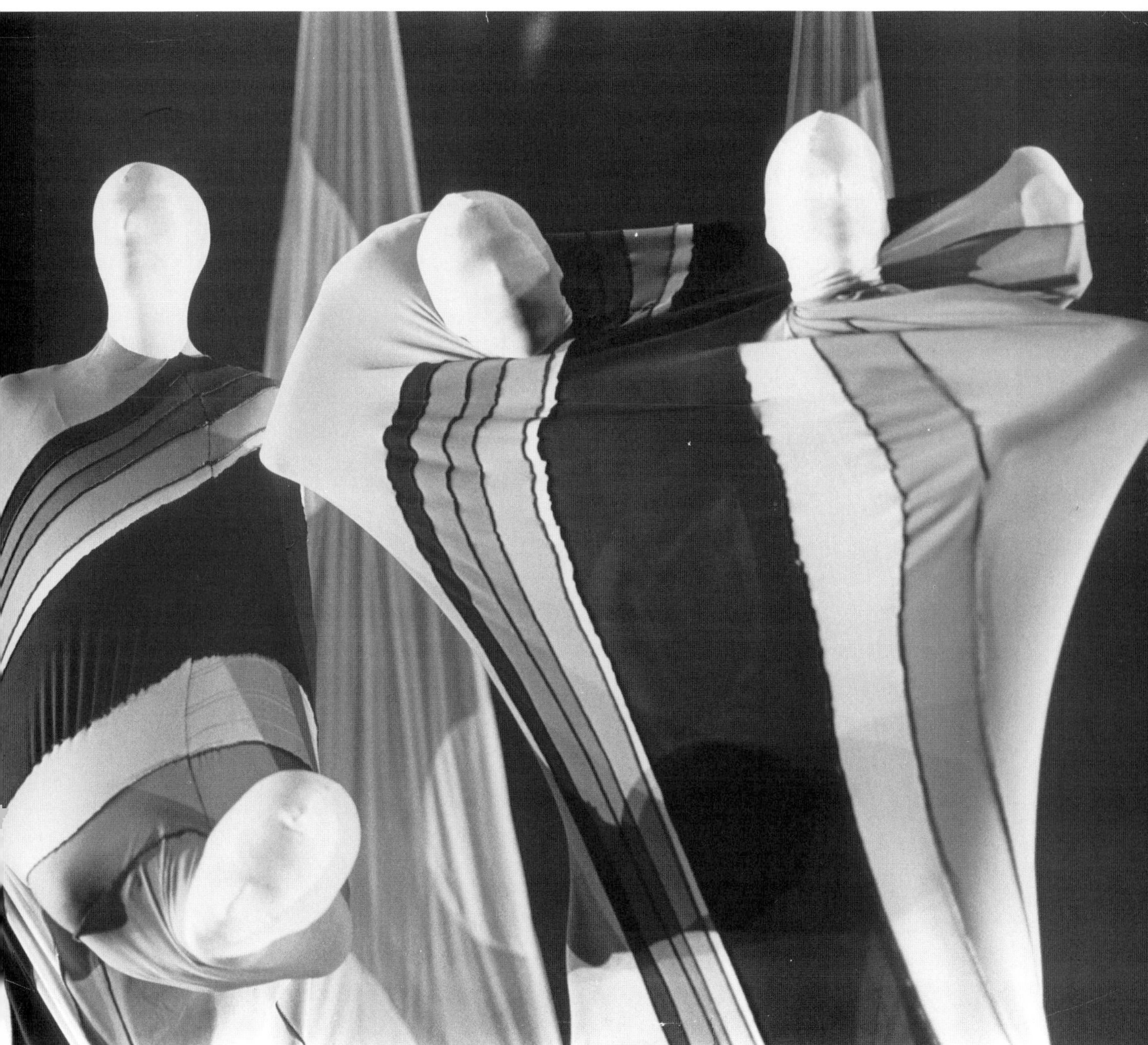

Milton Oleaga

such "natural" phenomena as a justification for a reevaluation of the undesirable ways people move their bodies simply because such motion is possible. "The spirit of Western man... made him think he had to work, to exert effort or force, and to conquer nature. Therefore dance teachers have passed on this erroneous notion about human movement — that you must 'make' the movement happen, or dominate the movement through your will, or through 'hard work.' "

Hawkins rejects the entire cycle of mechanistic dance technique which dominates ballet as well as modern dance and devotes himself to an elusive "natural movement." "The reason," he has stated, "one is filled with wonder at the movement of most animals, like the cat family, is that they are always concentric, effortless; they have never been taught a fallacious theory (of movement) which, out of a partialness of the human mind, has inculcated ideas... that man should glory in being excentered, filled with effort and striving and subtle Puritanism."

As a result of Hawkins' explorations of human motion, his dances evoke exactly the sense of wonder which we derive from watching the movement of animals. His works are holistic to such a degree that they possess the ceremonial atmosphere of nature itself. His dances so closely approach the flow of natural phenomena and are so filled with the pulse which lives beneath the apparent diversity of things that they epitomize the special meditative atmosphere and semblance of "meaning" which is the basis of Oriental poetry. Yet there is nothing even slightly Oriental about Hawkins' choreography. The title of his *Here and Now with Watchers* affirms the subtle brilliance of his highly individual vision — an eternal "now" which takes instantaneous shape in a world in which time experiences motion and motion experiences time, in which apparitions pass before us and produce the form of motion, and in which motion becomes suddenly visible in the bodies, in the grass, and in the countless things it momentarily sways in its ceaseless coming and going.

Three Ceremonial Grounds

Since the rebellion at the turn of the century, dance has had many dominant idioms, rather than a single one. At first, it was only a debate between ballet and modern dance. Gradually, larger questions emerged, especially as the interaction of the various "schools" of dancing became thorough. Ballet became highly influenced by the ideologies of various modern dancers, while modern dance showed many signs of the balletic emphasis upon precision, codified technique, and body line. In both modern dance and ballet, the dichotomy was equally based upon disparate techniques, as well as the question of just what dancing was supposed to be "about." In the political upheaval which followed the American Depression many modern dancers (and some ballet choreographers, such as Kurt Joos) became immersed in dances of social criticism. The Dudley-Maslow-Bales Dance Trio, as well as Anna Sokolow, made their first impact in political dance-dramas. Other choreographers rejected social content as inartistic and, like Graham, pursued psychological themes based on Greek mythology or American legends.

The narrative style preoccupied the first generation of modern dancers. At the same time, ballet divided its emphasis between old-fashioned pantomimic fairytales, the large symphonic works of Leonide Massine, and the plotless dances of

In Erick Hawkins' *Ritual of the Descent* there is a rediscovery of fundamentality.

A. John Geraci

Lois Greenfield

The Erick Hawkins Dance Company in *Death Is the Hunter.*

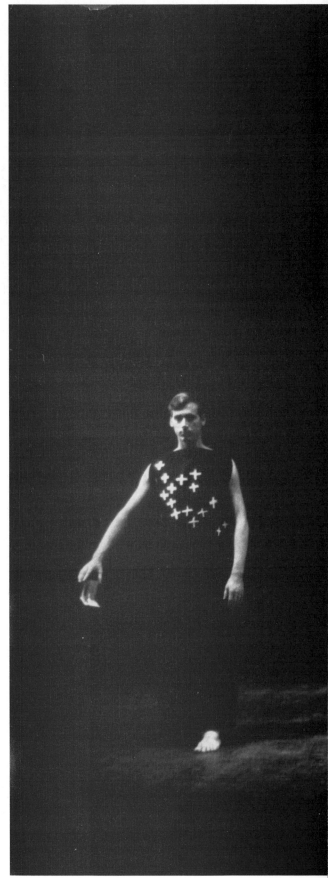

There is a celebration of the natural world in *The Milky Way* from *Black Lake* performed by the Erick Hawkins Company.

Ted Yaple

George Balanchine. The purely technical debate of ballet versus modern dance aside, the major issue involved the content of dancing. Two schools grew out of the second generation of choreographers committed to the Graham-Humphrey-Weidman evolutionary, dramatic, and ritualistic dance-drama — notably Paul Taylor, José Limón, Jerome Robbins, Antony Tudor, Glenn Tetley, Anna Sokolow (to name a few on the East Coast), and Lester Horton and the San Francisco Contemporary Dancers, principally on the West Coast. Of course, Martha Graham remained the leading choreographer of the dramatic idiom, but her influence was challenged by two dancers from her own company and by a theater director from the Henry Street Settlement Playhouse in New York. The opposition was built on an idiom of abstract, nonobjective dance which disavowed dramatic motives as passé in favor of the use of movement for its own sake. The major advocates of this alternative style were Merce Cunningham, Erick Hawkins, and Alwin Nikolais — as well as George Balanchine, whose popularity as a creator of plotless ballets helped to justify the pursuit of abstraction in modern dance.

Plains Daybreak, 1982, a ritual drama with choreographer Erick Hawkins as First Man and Douglas Andersen as Buffalo.

David Fullard

Randy Howard in *Plains Daybreak* by Erick Hawkins, 1979. According to Anna Kisselgoff of *The New York Times,* it is a "metaphorical essay, perhaps the most perfect one in the Hawkins repertory," deeply rooted in the ceremonial dances of American Indians.

Somewhere beyond and between these two poles is the robust avant-garde which emerged during the sixties and seventies. Most of the exponents of this important idiom arose from the influences of Cunningham, Hawkins, and Nikolais — and in various ways they reject narrative dance in favor of highly idiosyncratic forms ranging from environmental works without audiences, participatory works which verge on therapy, dances stemming from naturalistic acts of daily life, performances of violent self-expression, and conceptual events which consist entirely of notifying an "audience" of an "event" by postcard.

The present and the future, to the extent that it can be envisioned, are propelled by some of the most dominant and distressing events of the twentieth century: the decline of all forms of public truth, the decay of political credibility, and the pervasive fatalism which is the result of the atom bombs which fell on Japan in 1945. Our art and, especially, our dances reflect all of these conditions. It is no wonder that there is confusion on the part of the lay audience, consternation on the part of conservative critics, and sublime anarchy among choreographers.

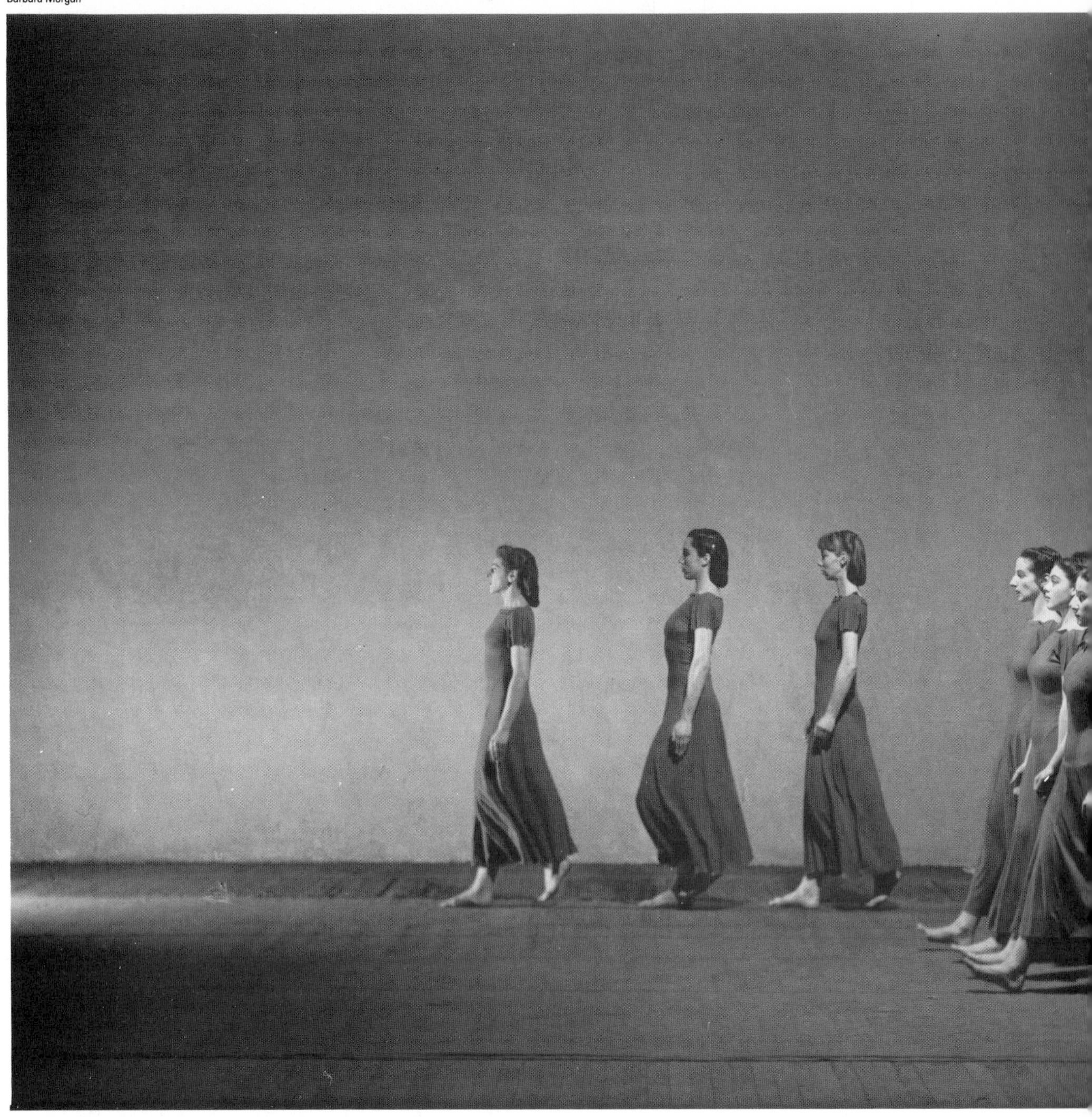

Primitive Mysteries, performed by the Martha Graham Dance Company in 1935, is probably the greatest work by Graham and a seminal achievement for the twentieth century.

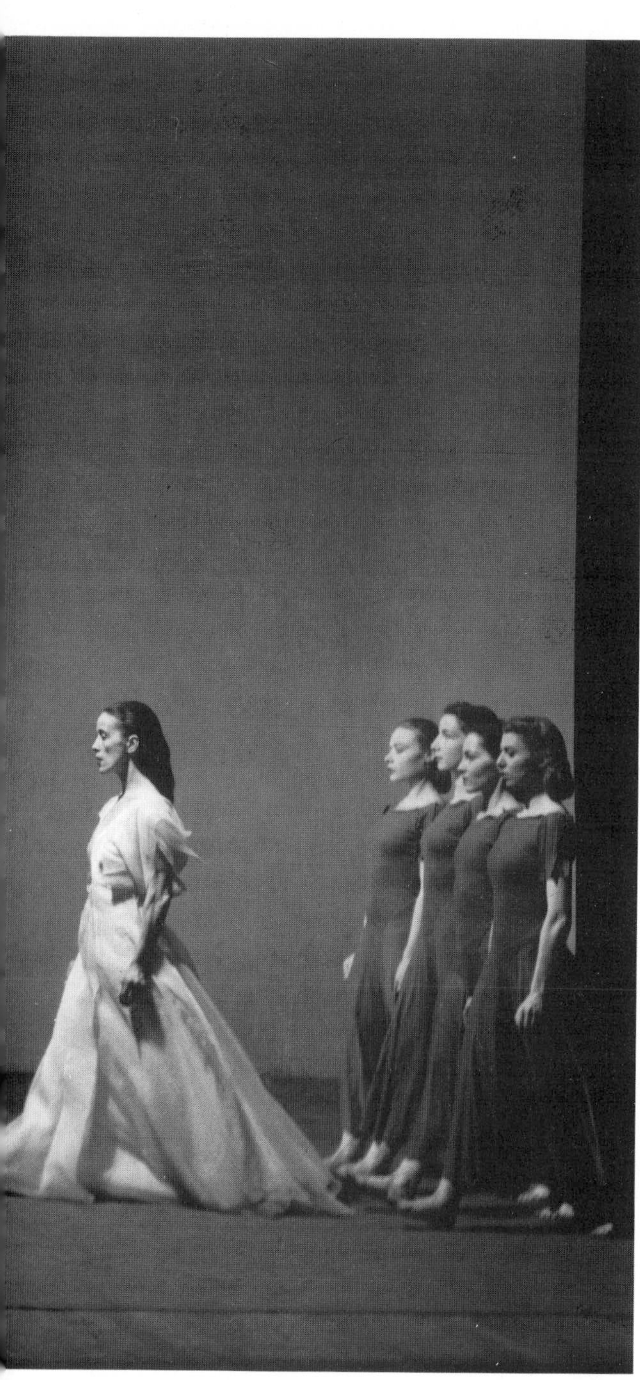

Charles Weidman and Ted Shawn forged new ideas about males in dance. Here Weidman in *Daddy Was a Fireman,* 1938.

Barbara Morgan

The Humphrey-Weidman Dance Company performs Weidman's master opus, *Lynchtown,* in 1938, an American political and dance manifesto.

Barbara Morgan

Barbara Morgan

An American transplant from the German school of Mary Wigman, Hanya Holm, pictured dancing in *Trend,* 1938, introduced the epic sensibility of dancing.

Doris Humphrey in *With My Red Fires,* 1938, launched the American renaissance of dance with Graham and Weidman.

From the second generation of American dancers, Valerie Bettis dances in *Desperate Heart,* 1944.

Barbara Morgan

Jean Erdman's landmark theater work, *The Coach with Six Insides*, based on James Joyce's *Finnegan's Wake*. (left to right) John Wallace-Wilson as Shem, Jean Erdman as Anna Livia Plurabelle, and Keith Druhl as Shaun, 1982.

Jean Erdman's *The Coach with Six Insides*, based on James Joyce's *Finnegan's Wake* with music by Teijo Ito, premiered in 1962. The original cast included (left to right) Leonard Frey, Jean Erdman, Sheila Roy, Van Dexter, and Anita Douglas.

courtesy Theater of the Open

courtesy Theater of the Open Eye

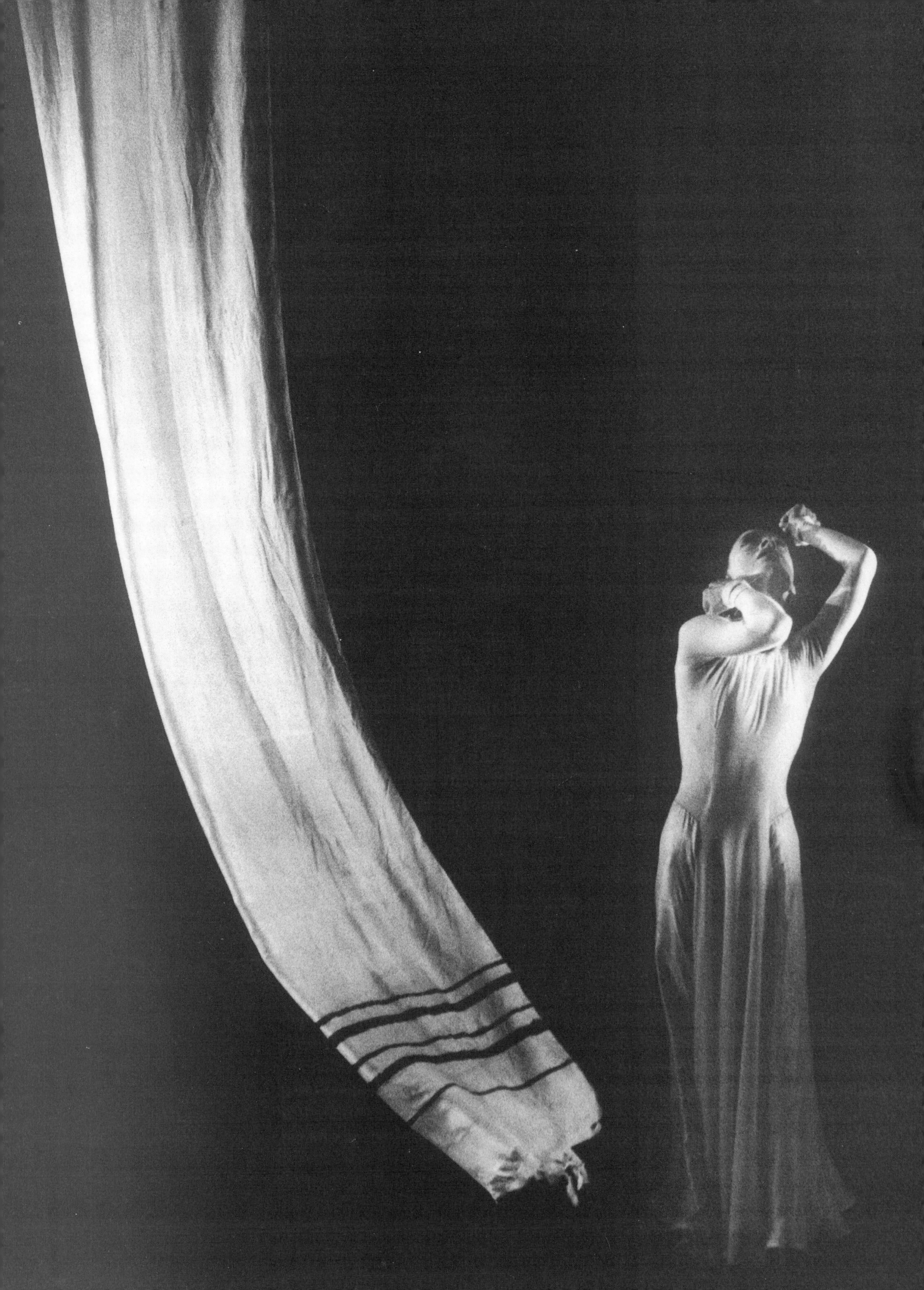

I do not know where to find in any literature, whether ancient or modern, any adequate account of that Nature with which I am personally acquainted.

— HENRY DAVID THOREAU,
The Journal

RITUAL AS ART

ART DOES NOT consciously come into existence until the values implicit in ritual are shattered by social change and must be manifested in the idiosyncratic works of individuals rather than the unified customs of tribes. When art arises out of ritual, it becomes self-conscious and is quickly surrounded by various artistic principles with which we make aesthetic judgments and which shape the definition of the purposes and techniques of art.

Art is usually concerned with "expressiveness" and with "something" which is expressed. But the criteria by which we once automatically knew what words like "expressiveness" meant have broken down as art has ventured into entirely new areas. So we have to try to redefine what we mean by expression and we have to decide what kinds of things are expressed in art.

A central issue of exploration in dance since 1900 has been an effort to define nonpantomimic movement. Intrinsic to that difficult definition is the question of how nonliteral, nonrepresentational movements convey "something" to an audience, whether that something is wholly abstract or thoroughly dramatic. The original ritualistic power of movement was ineffable — an inextricable aspect of tribalism — a nonliteral, nonlinear expression of unspoken group values which had no need of articulation because they were fundamental to the experience of the entire tribe. We are now emerging from a long period during which it was assumed that anything of importance could be named in specific words or in specific gestures, such as pantomime. Recently, Jerome Robbins

arl Lang in *The Possessed*

epitomized the new sensibility when he said that "the world I'm interested in is the one where things are not named." These unnamed "things" have become progressively central to the aims of most choreographers. Through a renewal of certain ritual processes the ineffable has become visible in dance once again. By what means do choreographers achieve the materialization of nonrepresentational things — of *apparitions* — in their dances?

Isadora Duncan provided the first answer to that question. Though her dancing has often been accused of rampant self-expression, in actuality Duncan was concerned with an impersonal expressiveness contained within and conveyed by pure movement without reference to plot, dramatic characterization, or motivational psychology. Duncan suggested a principle which revised the naturalistic aims of Noverre and Fokine and stressed the return to abstract, rather than narrative, dancing. The critical stance of Duncan and her followers grew out of their efforts to give an expressional character to dance which was generic to its basic forms. This was something ballet at the close of the nineteenth century has failed to achieve. By now it is apparent that Duncan's influences were not limited to modern dance; ballet was also radically changed by her ideas.

Duncan was a contemporary of Sigmund Freud, and one of the results of their combined impact on art was self-expressive manipulation of personal, psychological history. This *inwardness* occurred in all the arts at a time when communal values were no longer capable of supporting the "public truth" which prior generations of artists have used as the substantiating dogma for expressional content in their art. Duncan, however, was not interested in the self as psyche as much as she was interested in the self as body. Despite her free-flowing dance, the subsequent history of dance from 1900 to 1960 shows a dominant effort — in the name of Isadora — to evolve from abstract movement to narrative movement in which plot and characters are central issues. This process completely reversed the trend found in all the other arts which were moving at that time from imitative realism to abstraction. Ironically, this tendency toward explicitness in dance was reversed during the sixties and seventies. Just as painting, for instance, was renewing an interest in representational realism, dance was rejecting objective content.

The situation of content and expressiveness in dance has become highly problematical. If Jerome Robbins was correct when he said that dance is a form in which things are never named, then what do we dance about?

What Is Expressiveness?

When dance critic John Martin axiomatized the neuromuscular basis of dance, he stated only half the truth: "Any emotional state tends to express itself in movements which may not be practically useful or in any way representational, but nevertheless reflects the specific character and quality of that emotional state. Thus, at the root of all the varied manifestations of dancing, lies the common impulse to resort to movement to externalize emotional states which we cannot externalize by rational means. The dancer utilizes the principle that every emotional state tends to express itself in movement, and that the movements thus created spontaneously, though they are not representational, reflect accurately in each case the character of the particular emotional state. Because of the inherent contagion of bodily movement, which makes

Milton Oleaga

Martha Graham's *Phaedra,* 1962.

onlookers feel sympathetically in their own musculature the exertions they see in somebody else's musculature, the dancer is able to convey through movement the most intangible emotional experience."

Martin — like Fokine and Noverre — was tied down to the literal, dramatic tradition of dance. His description of the neuromuscular transaction is biased in favor of a dramatic interpretation of dance, and this view has made the evolution of abstract, concert dancing problematical. To judge from what Martin wrote, *all* dance resorts to movement to externalize emotional states, and *all* dancers wish to convey through movement the most intangible emotional experience. This simply is not true. Or at least Martin's terminology creates confusion.

The problem here is not the neuromuscular transaction which John Martin described; the problem is found in his description of it — for dancing is not concerned fundamentally with *emotional states* or *emotional experience* any more than music is. These constant references to emotion in dance during the 1930s

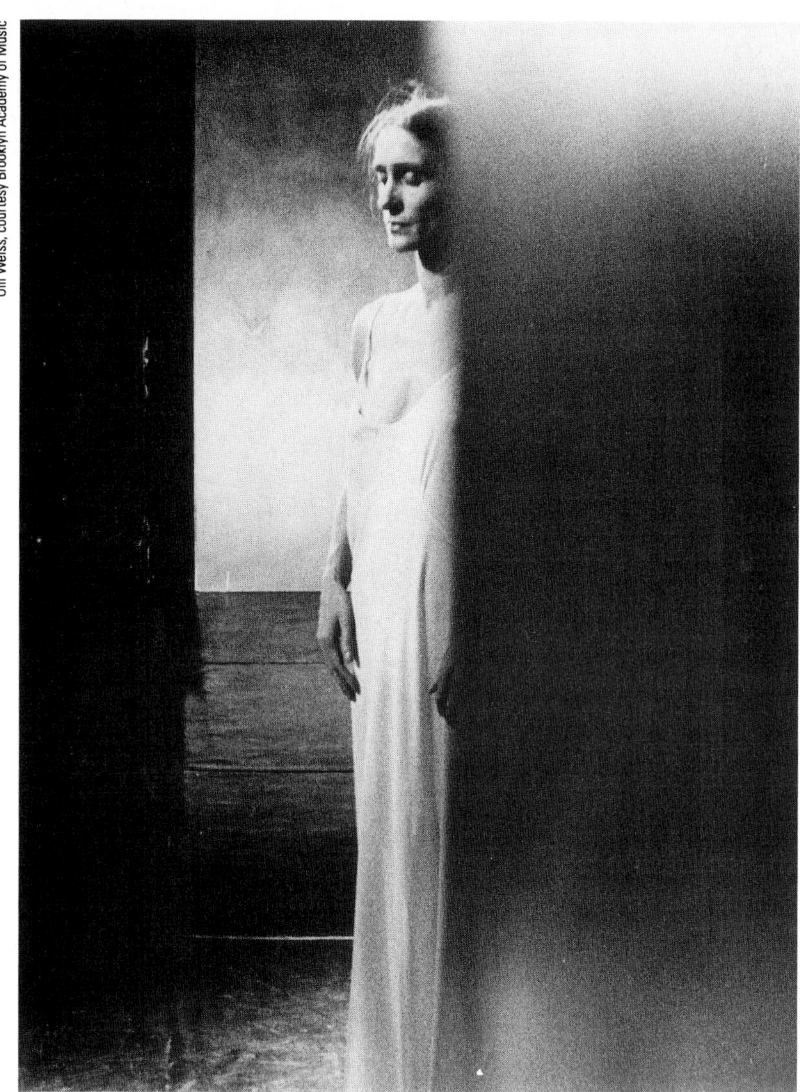
Ulli Weiss, courtesy Brooklyn Academy of Music

Pina Bausch in *Cafe Muller,* an important work in the repertory of West Germany's major experimental theater company, the Pina Bausch Wuppertaler Tanztheater.

and 1940s now necessitate a qualification of terms. Is dance really emotional? What do we mean by emotion? Does the presence of emotion in dance necessarily make dance a dramatic form? And if emotion exists as part of the nature of dance, specifically what kinds of emotion are intrinsic to dance as an art form?

American philosopher Susanne Langer, who is greatly concerned with art as an expression of feeling, has suggested that what we mean by feeling in art is *expressiveness* — but not emotion.

"Expressiveness," she writes in *Problems in Art*, "is the same in all art works. A work of art is an expressive form, and what it expresses is human feeling. But the word 'feeling' must be taken here in its broadest sense, meaning *everything that can be felt*, from physical sensation, pain and comfort, excitement and repose, to the most complex emotions, intellectual tensions, or the steady feeling-tones of a conscious human life."

It is important to recognize the subtle revision of the definition of emotion which occurs in Langer's remarks — "*everything that can be felt*" represents both a physical and intellectual potential, both physical sensation and intellectual tension. Emotion in art has nothing necessarily in common with the rampage of the private psyche. It is not confined to lavish displays of personal emotion or to

nda Kent and Nicholas Gunn in the Paul Taylor Dance Company's production of *Runes*.

the imitation of dramatic events. It is not restricted to the physical depiction of psychological events but can also deal with the transactions of the abstract imagination.

What Langer is talking about is *sentience* and not mere emotionality. Contemporary choreographers agree with Langer and reject the notion that feeling and thought are incompatible.

"Abstract thinking," she has stated in her book, *Philosophical Sketches*, "is traditionally treated as incompatible with emotional response. Were our rationality purely an increase of automatic processes, emotions would really be the sheer disturbances they are often taken to be. But if it is true that abstraction is made by the joint functions of perceptual and emotional mechanisms, then we are faced with the paradoxical finding that only highly emotional creature could have developed a talent for abstract thought. . . . Whatever there is in experience that is not discursively communicable is unspeakable, ineffable; and according to practically all serious philosophical theories today, is unknowable. Yet there is a great deal of experience that is knowable but defies discursive formulation, and therefore defies verbal expression: that is what we sometimes call the *subjective aspect* of experience." It is precisely this subjective aspect of experience that is what is meant by the word "sentience."

The core of dancing, the neuromuscular activity of the human body, is one of the vehicles by which sentience becomes visible. And the "emotional states which express themselves in movement," to which John Martin referred in his definition of dancing, are examples of sentience which is manipulated artistically, with or without dramatic purpose. The spectrum of the expressive potential of dance is extremely wide: from a naturalistic statement of emotional and physical facts in strict chronological sequence (Tudor's *Pillar of Fire*, for example), a realistic composition divested of particulars (Graham's *Appalachian Spring*), a surrealistic work which develops in terms of the sequence of emotion but not the sequence of naturalistic events (Robbins' *The Cage*), to an abstract dance which conveys only a semblance of human behavior (Balanchine's *Serenade* or Cunningham's *Rainforest*).

The major objection of choreographers of the sixties and seventies to dance which is explicitly dramatic is that this kind of narrative dancing puts too much stress upon subject matter and too little stress upon the properties and potentials of dance itself. In their view, sentience is not subject matter in dance but rather an indispensable source of power.

After long debate about the expressiveness of dance and its expressive content, there are still choreographers who create dance-dramas which depict dramatic situations; there are still those who reject all semblance of personality in dancing; and there are also those involved in radical realism in which screaming, groveling, and howling at near-lunatic intensity are used to produce shock in the audience. This debate cannot be resolved, but any definition of expressiveness in dance must somehow strive to be large enough to contain all these diverse attitudes.

Such a widely inclusive viewpoint has not been typical of dance theory in the past. There has usually been far more concern for narrative dance than for dances which do not involve plot, incidents, or characters. An important lesson in this regard can be learned from the history of opera, insofar as it is a medium in

The San Francisco Contemporary Dancers sustained a rich dance tradition with its own works and those of guest companies for over a decade. Here are the company's Glenna Shaw and James Croshaw in *A Season in Hell.*

Jean Mathis and Raymond Evans of the San Francisco Contemporary Dancers in *Yerma.*

Diana Russell and the author in *The Tree of Night* by the San Francisco Contemporary Dancers.

Chic Lloyd

alph Hampton

Ralph Hampton

L. D. Vartoogian

Aileen Cropley and Rudolph Nureyev in Paul Taylor's *Aureole*.

which there have been several traditions, rather than a single tradition, and the development of these contrasting idioms of opera indicate the potential for great diversity not usually recognized in the dance world. In the past exceptionally little attention has been given to the kind of abstract dancing which is performed on concert stages. In the history of opera we discover that both the dramatic and the nondramatic traditions have been provided with prominent places in the opera house.

Opera began toward the end of the sixteenth century, and its development was divided between the effort of two pioneers: Christophe Willibald Gluck, who forged a natural, theatrical idiom, and Nikolaus Hasse, who created vocal music which emphasized classical conventions and lavish ornamentation.

According to many musicologists, the evolution of opera was thwarted by a dichotomy between its musical considerations and its concern for dramatic plot.

Music requires repetition and development, which tends to slow down dramatic action; plot requires continuity and rapid progression, which tends to cramp the development of music. The musical and dramatic elements of opera do not effectively serve one another.

The dramatic basis of an opera is its libretto. The music consists of various orchestral overtures and interludes which sum up and anticipate the dramatic action. It is also composed of various arias, duets, trios, and quartets in which the vocal aspect is developed and the orchestra plays a secondary, supportive role. Often the dramatic intentions of an opera libretto are carried forward by spoken dialogue or recitative. Verdi's *Il Trovatore* or *Rigoletto* are examples of this kind of conventional opera.

A music-drama, in contrast, tends to use the human voice as an integral part of the orchestral texture and to create a more thoroughly dramatic work in which separate arias and duets, etc., are not permitted to break the progress of the drama. Orchestral writing normally plays a greater role in music-drama. Repeated motifs representing aspects of the action or characters are used as the basis for the kind of development and recapitulation which is primary to musical composition. Wagner's *Tristan und Isolde* is an example of music-drama. Wagner wrote extensive essays to justify his departure from operatic tradition.

Though music-drama is often used as the model for new musical works by modern composers, opera is still very much alive. In other words, music-drama has not replaced opera; they coexist as expressions of two widely separate aesthetic viewpoints.

"Ballet" is a term which readily describes a dance style very much like opera. "Dance-drama" parallels music-drama. In other words, the development of ballet in the court of Louis XIV approximated a genre like opera: it had strict conventions; it used pantomime to further plot much as opera used dialogue or recitative; it organized choreographic "arias," "duets," and "trios," etc., which stressed pure dance and which were tucked between the expository, pantomimic action. Ballet also makes elaborate use of ornamentation and technical daring which suggests the style of opera called *bel canto*. *Giselle*, *Swan Lake*, and *Sleeping Beauty* are typical of this type of ballet.

Dance-drama, like music-drama, gives its entire emphasis to methods which further the dramatic action and atmosphere of the dance but does so with a concentrated use of the drama implicit in gesture. The music which accompanies a dance-drama is generally more "musical" and less supportive; it challenges the attention of the audience and often runs its own independent course rather than simply marking time for the dancers. Gesture is more freely evolved and developed than it is in traditional ballet. Solos and *pas de deux*, etc., are integrated into the basic choreographic flow of the dance and contribute to the dramatic continuity. The sequence of the "plot" is often nonlinear and departs from naturalism much as contemporary plays and novels shun naturalistic causality. The dramatic outline of a dance-drama is likely to be fundamentally reshaped from the realistic viewpoint into a ritualistic form. Martha Graham's *Circe*, José Limón's *Moor's Pavane*, and Jerome Robbins' *Watermill* are examples of dance-drama.

Ballet and dance-drama are only two examples of the vast potential spectrum of dance. They have no more exclusive right to be considered the definitive forms of dance than opera and music-drama have in the broad field of music. But ballet,

Johan Elbers

Paul Sarasardo, Michelle Rebaud, and Jacques Patarozzi in the Paul Sarasardo Dance Company's *The Path*.

first, and then dance-drama have had such an inordinately dominant impact on choreographers, dancers, and audiences that for a long time it was quite impossible to compose any other kind of dance. Thus, abstract choreography, a dance form that is essentially without a "libretto," managed to surface only with great difficulty. For the sake of convenience I am going to call this kind of dancing "concert dance."

Concert dance is concerned with the arrangement and development of gestures without explicit dramatic purposes, plot, or characters. The only subject matter of concert dance is gesture itself. This does not mean that concert dance must depend solely upon technical skill to make an impact or that it is incapable of rousing a wide variety of responses in an audience. Quite the contrary. The impact of concert dance, however, is based upon an expressiveness which exists within gesture, within movement itself and not in the maneuvers of plot. Balanchine's *Agon*, Nikolais' *Imago*, Cunningham's *Winterbranch*, and Humphrey's *Air for the G String* are examples of concert dance.

What Do Dances Express?

Behind all forms of dance — ballet, dance-drama, and concert dance — is a common expressive impulse. But expressiveness is not a single, uniform power in any art. It constantly changes, at least on a certain level, as public values change. What is amusing to one era is not necessarily amusing to another. What is tragic to one age is not necessarily tragic to another. The quality of sentience changes from one era to the next, and in ways so subtle that even the most undefinable qualities of life — those which have no direct relationship to "emotions" — also evolve and change.

It is relatively simple to conceive how public values make their various, constantly changing appearances in the works of novelists, playwrights, painters, and sculptors, but it is more difficult to imagine how public values can have any relationship to something as abstract as, for instance, instrumental music or concert dance. But they do.

The romanticism of a Tchaikovsky symphony, though built entirely of abstract notes and having no apparent "plot" or program, nonetheless seems lugubrious to the nonromantic mentality. The transparency and meticulous development of a baroque sonata may seem redundant, fussy, and inarticulate to a listener devoted to serial music. On the other hand, the musical mind of Anton Webern often seems morbid, remote, and ugly to a classically oriented listener who has a melodic expectation of music. Public values are so fundamental to human responsiveness that they reach into even the so-called mathematical abstraction of absolute music.

Social values have always had an impact upon the character of a work of art and still do. But today that impact has become uncertain because we live in an age in which there is no longer one truth but many, not one school of art but many; and people are being presented with a constantly increasing number of ways to think of, look at, and evaluate the same thing.

In a book which definitively summed up the impact of this condition on fiction between 1918 and 1945, John Aldridge commented: "One cannot speak of fiction without sooner or later speaking of values." The subject of values in art is by now a familiar subject of discussion, but in Aldridge's day it was, perhaps, better grasped than it is today.

Art cannot exist without evaluation, and evaluation cannot exist without values. The simplest human comment, gesture, or intonation carries with it an expressed or implied evaluation. Even people who insist that they believe in nothing, and who claim that they produce works which revel in nothingness, are expressing an evaluation of experience. We simply cannot do *anything* without expressing *something*. "If love died," Aldridge commented in reference to the artists of the post-World War I Lost Generation, "they stopped believing in love and began believing in sex. If everything collapsed and they were left with nothing, that too was all right. They began believing in nothing."

The predicament of expression in the arts was the subject of another critic, David Daiches, who stated in *The Novel and the Modern World*: "It is public truth which provides the artist with his means of communication. It enables him to communicate emotion [sentience] and attitude by simply describing incidents; it gives him a storehouse of symbols with guaranteed responses; it enables him to construct a plot by selecting the patterning events which, on this public criterion, are significant.... One of the most outstanding features of Western civilization in the twentieth century has been the drying-up of traditional sources of value and the consequent decay of uniform belief.... New developments in psychology arrived very opportunely and encouraged artists to beg the question of value by confining their world to the limits of an individual mind and assessing value solely in terms of the consciousness of that mind. James Joyce's *Ulysses* is a prime example of this trend."

We can also use this principle in discussing dance. *Swan Lake*, for instance, for all its naïveté, is the depiction of incidents which, in 1895, possessed the storehouse of symbols which elicited guaranteed responses from its audience. Marius Petipa and Lev Ivanov constructed *Swan Lake* by selecting and patterning events and characters that were significant in terms of the public values of their day. Public truth provided Petipa and Ivanov with the basis of their theatrical communication. It enabled them to convey attitudes and

Two Penny Portrait is performed by the Louis Falco Dance Company's Louis Falco and Georgiana Holmes.

feelings by simply describing incidents. The form and technique of *Swan Lake* were also products of a public criterion and of a storehouse of symbols with guaranteed responses: because public truth also dictates public taste and therefore establishes the techniques which result in the purely mechanical aspects of skill in art. The same values which gave credence and emotive validity to the events and characters of *Swan Lake* also induced a style and a technique generically related to the values and events of the ballet. The form of expression operates on the same values as the subject of a work of art. Odette in *Swan Lake* is a combination of balletic steps and pantomime. The steps and pantomime describe the Swan Queen as clearly as she is described by the literal events in which she participates in the ballet. The steps, spatial and temporal forms, plot, and characters of *Swan Lake* are interactive and interdependent. Together they constitute *Swan Lake* and together they also epitomize their era. This process is called tradition — but, contrary to conservative judgment, it is constantly and erratically changing and not fixed or forever evolving toward a single, predetermined destiny.

Milton Oleaga

The great Mexican-American dancer-choreographer, José Limón, produced a marvelous and unique stage presence. With Erick Hawkins, Limón founded a whole new basis for the male participation in dance, while, at the same time, he infused his work with elements of his Mexican-American traditions. Here Limón performs in *The Traitor.*

This discussion of *Swan Lake* brings attention to plot and characters, but it does not mean the impact of public values on art depends upon a literal, dramatic framework. To the contrary, concert dance is as much affected by public truths as ballet, though it is apparently devoid of plot, characters, emotions, and any such concern with it. The value system of a society operates on every level — some of its manifestations are subtle and are expressive in an entirely nonliteral, nonlinear way.

It is true that we cannot produce in music a *direct* emotional statement, yet there has not been an era in which "feeling" was not associated with the most abstract elements of musical composition. These abstract elements are not fixed and consistent; they constantly change as the values of the world change. Music is not so absolute that it stands aloof from the era which produces it. Music reflects the public truth of its age through sentience — without which it simply could not be art. What is true of absolute music is also true of absolute dance — or concert dance.

The psychological work of art (in dance and literature, etc.) is a method of dealing with personality without confronting the value system of society. This is achieved, as David Daiches has said, by dealing with "the limits of an individual mind and assessing value solely in terms of the consciousness of that mind." In dance-drama there are psychological works such as Tudor's *Pillar of Fire*.

The psychological art required alterations of technique and form. Tudor, therefore, devised an original mode of gesture and revised balletic vocabulary, making it more flexible and more capable of reflecting complex internal rather than simplistic external events. Tudor's dance-dramas were outside the tradition of *Swan Lake*, not only in terms of his creation of a dance-drama rather than a ballet but also in the structures and gestures of his dance. In subtle ways, Tudor altered the expressive tone of gesture. In his day, it would have been unlikely for him to choreograph another *Swan Lake*. The public truth which had justified and motivated *Swan Lake* was no longer viable or visible in Antony Tudor's world. Psychology had caught the interest and faith of society. Artists were thinking in terms of the stream of consciousness which motivated most external actions. Tudor considered the motivational inner world to be real and the external world

Yvonne Rainer and dancers in *Performance 1972*, which represents a crisis in dancing: a reappraisal in light of the real world.

Babette Mangolte

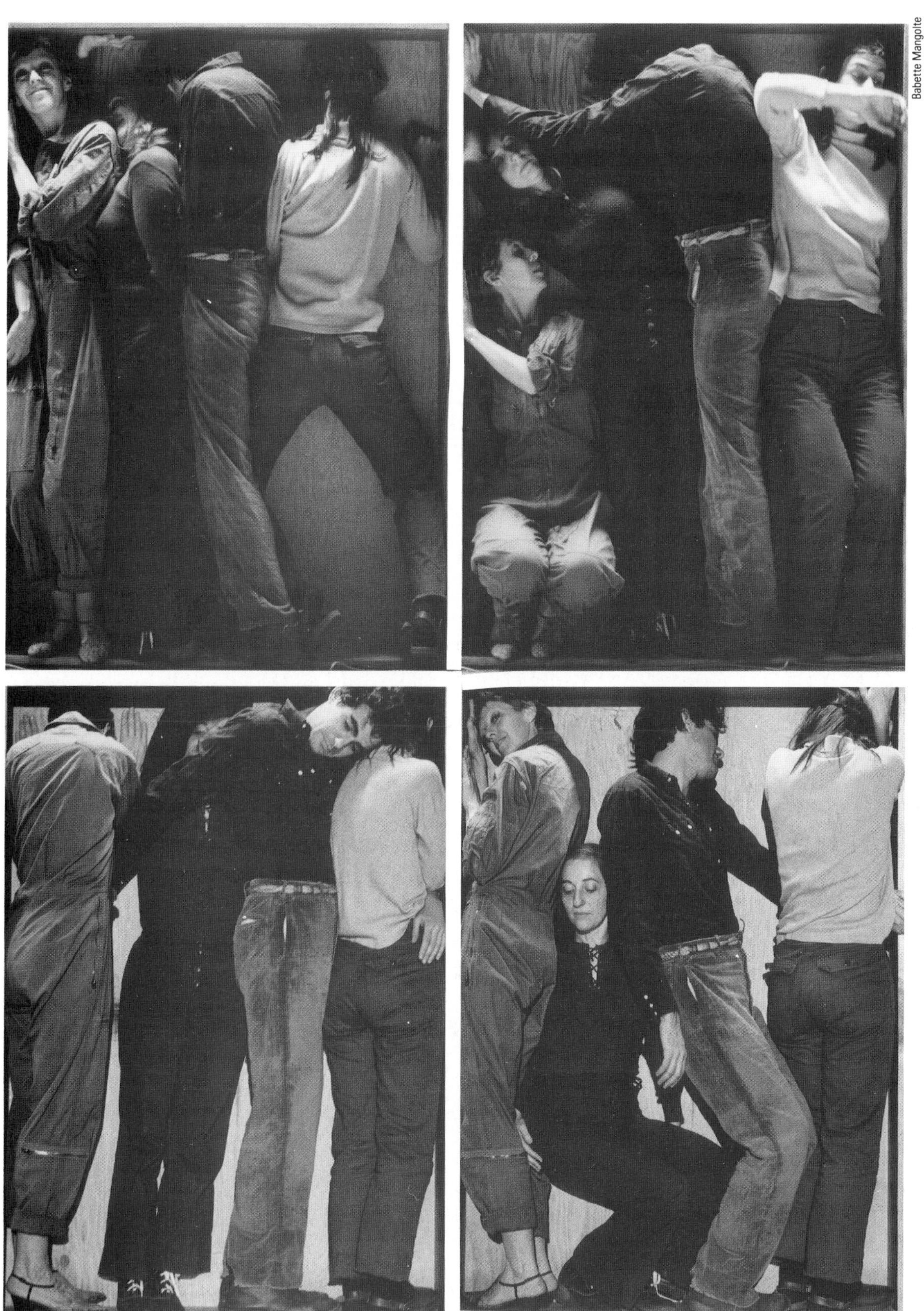

Babette Mangolte

A composite photograph from Yvonne Rainer's *Performance 1972*.

a mere reflection of it. A dancer in a Tudor dance-drama is a very special kind of performer — so different from dancers who perform the roles of Odette or Giselle that they seem to belong to a totally different order. In a Tudor dance-drama, the dancers cannot convey the public truth of their world by behaving like Odette any more than James Joyce's Molly Bloom could exist if she spoke in the prose of Charles Dickens.

Expression in dance is indistinct from content. But what is more important is that technique merges with content. When artists' values require them to convey something new in their work, then new techniques become necessary. This is as true in dance as it is in fiction and painting. Technology originally justified the Western idea of the separation of content and technique; at the same time, it ultimately required the revision of that dichotomy.

This controversy of the relationship of technique and content was described by Mark Schorer in his famous essay "Technique as Discovery": "Modern criticism has demonstrated with finality that in art, beauty and truth are indivisible and one. The Keatsian overtones of these terms are mitigated and an old dilemma is solved if for beauty we substitute form, and for truth, content. We

Yvonne Rainer and Company in *Story of a Woman Who...*, 1973.

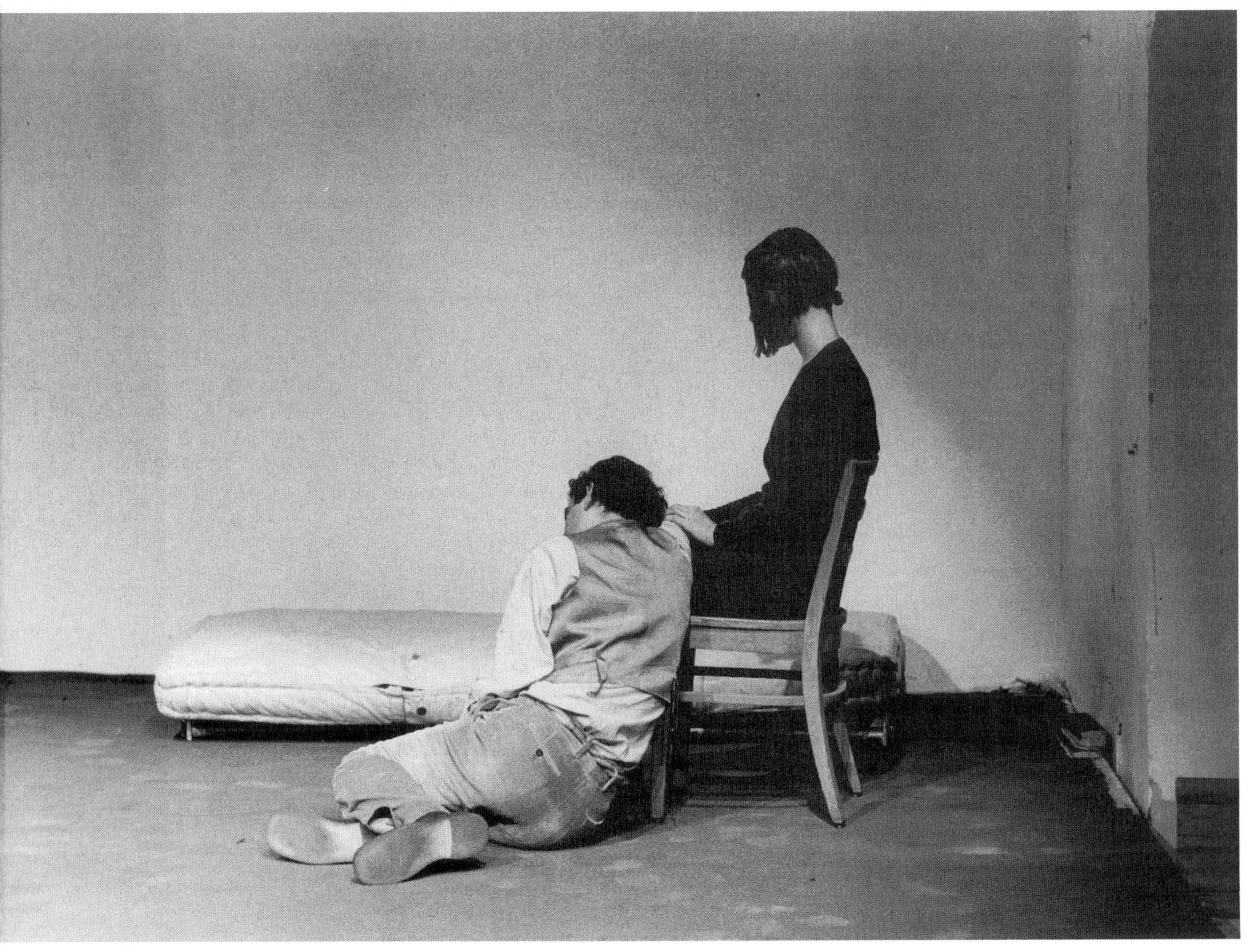

Babette Mangolte

Johan Elbers

Jeffrey Urban of the Rudy Perez Dance Company performs in *Colorado Rambler*, 1975.

Johan Elbers

Rudy Perez in *Running Board for a Native*, 1974.

Lois Greenfield

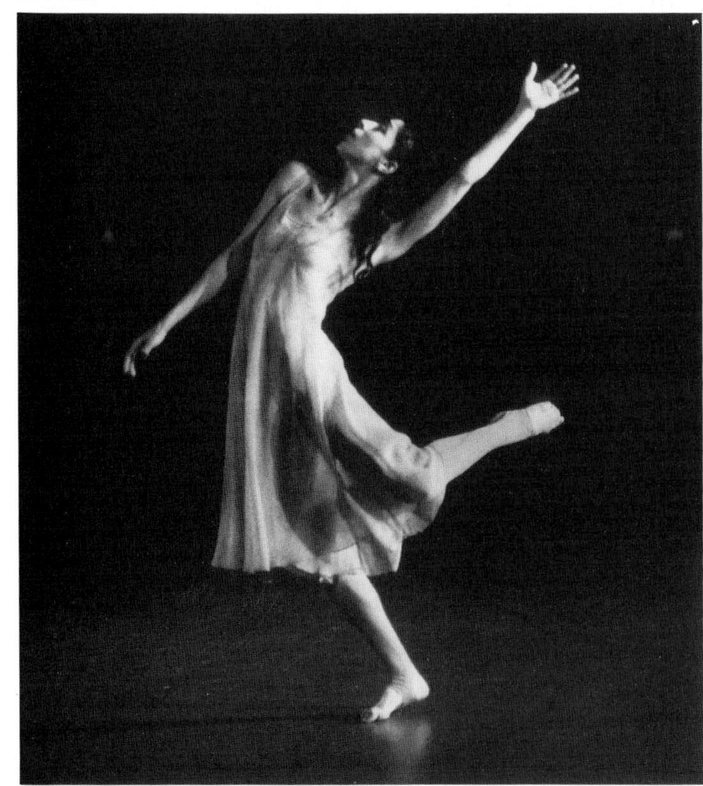

In Merce Cunningham's *Travelogue* there is a galvanic spirit in the exploration of the realities underlying dance.

Ze'eva Cohen in James Waring's *32 Variations in C Minor.*

Twyla Tharp in *Sue's Leg.*

courtesy WNET/PBS

Johan Elbers

Johan Elbers

New objects in dance can be seen in the Gus Solomons Dance Company's performance of *Ascent* from *Molehill*, danced by Gus Solomons, Jr.

may, without risk of loss, narrow them even more, and speak of technique and subject matter. Modern criticism has shown us that to speak of content as such is not to speak of art at all, but of experience; and that it is only when we speak of the *achieved* content, the form, the work of art as a work of art, that we speak as critics. The difference between content, or experience, and achieved content, or art, is technique. . . . Technique alone *objectifies* the materials of art; hence, technique alone evaluates these materials."

Schorer's final sentence recalls Susanne Langer. The artist, Langer stated, "formulates that elusive aspect of reality that is commonly taken to be amorphous and chaotic; that is, he *objectifies* the subjective realm."

Art is an objective expression in the form of technique. The imagination of an artist does not arbitrarily invent forms. His art is not *driven* by emotions. The artist selects an aspect of the reality he perceives. This process of selection is also a process of objectification. Once we, as audience, have entered into the artist's perception we are able to look on the world with the artist's "eyes." Art represents a distinction between the objective and the subjective, the representational and private expressivity. The Parthenon frieze or Bach's *B Minor Mass*, Michelangelo's Sistine Chapel or a poem by Leopardi, a quartet by Beethoven or a novel by Dostoyevsky are neither representational nor expressional. They are symbolic in

The Five Day Lobby Event performed by the Gus Solomons Dance Company in 1973 at the Massachusetts Institute of Technology represents the new environments used in dance.

Lois Greenfield

(Above and right) Nancy Meehan's brilliant composition, *Cloud . . . Roots,* 1984. An essay in sensuality and birth.

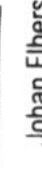
Johan Elbers

How much is enough? Trisha Brown and Carmen Beuchat of the Trisha Brown Dance Company perform *Pamplona Stones*, 1974.

a unique and fascinating way. They are not momentary outbursts of passion — they reveal a deep human grasp of unity and continuity. Such works of art are objective interpretations, not naïve imitations of reality. They are sentient forms, not an overflow of powerful private feelings. They are, above all else, the products of masterful technique — *whatever* the nature of that technique may be.

It is fashionable to explain nonobjective art as a method of indulging in technique for its own sake, rather than facing the emergence of values in our time. This criticism is off target. Nonobjective art has constructed a valid expressiveness built upon the postindustrial aesthetic potentials of technology itself. As history is a proper subject for the historical novel, technology is a proper focus of a work in which technique is the prime mover. The assumption that technology is stoical is unfounded, just as it is unfounded to assume that an abstract musical term like *allegro* has no meaning beyond the physics of sound. I earlier quoted John Aldridge's notion that if man were faced by the collapse of everything, he would actively believe in nothing. In a special and positive sense, nonobjective art — like concert dance — is a belief in "nothing."

The stronghold of nonobjective concepts in dance is concert dance. It is difficult, however, to imagine dancing which is created without reference to objects, since dance must be performed by dancers. The presence of dancers, even when they are highly dehumanized by costumes and makeup, automatically introduces a human as well as an objective element. Whether we are talking about classic ballet, dance-drama, or concert dance, one factor remains constant — the human body is implicit in dance, and with the body come associations and feelings which are inevitably part of any dance whether the choreographer likes it or not. What differentiates ballet, dance-drama, and concert dance are the meth-

Johan Elbers

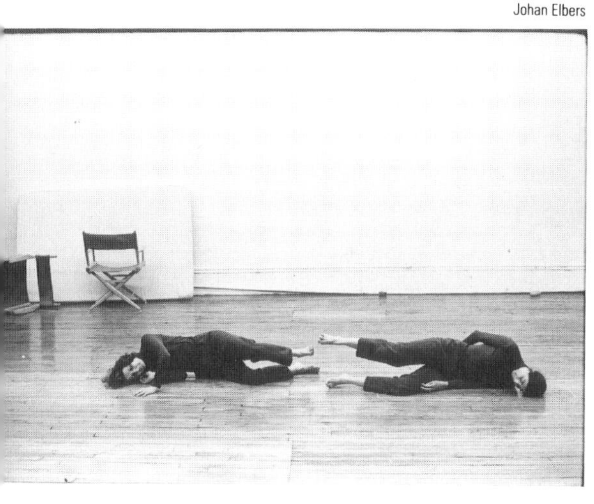

Trisha Brown and dancers use the real world in *Roof Piece,* 1973.

Babette Mangolte

Trisha Brown in *Accumulation Pieces,* 1973.

ods used to deal with the associations which the human body brings with it to a dance. In ballet the use of *literal* pantomime closes the gap between naïve realism and the things the body intimates by its very presence in a dance. In short, ballet exploits the fact that a prior era of faith has left a residue which can be resurrected by using pantomime as a means of representing sentimentality, and the values connected with it. Dance-drama recasts naïve realism in terms of ritual, so that the specific is generalized and the relationship of various sequences of gesture is based on psychological rather than material causation. Concert dance generalizes even further, so that dance sequences which seem to have a momentary relationship to an explicit feeling abruptly change into other sequences which do not seem in the least emotionally related to what came before. This constantly happens in the dances of Merce Cunningham; it also happens in the films of Michelangelo Antonioni.

Johan Elbers

Nathaniel Tileston

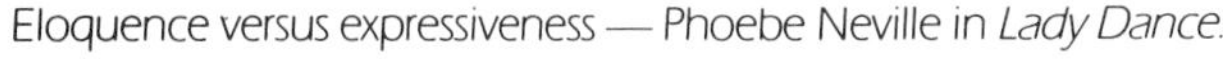

Eloquence versus expressiveness — Phoebe Neville in *Lady Dance*.

Phoebe Neville in *Memory*, 1975.

Trisha Brown and dancers in *Locust*, 1975.

New space, new time, and new dance can be seen in *Spiral*, 1974, by Trisha Brown and dancers.

Babette Mangolte

Johan Elbers

The Viola Farber Dance Company in *Lead Us Not into Penn Station,* 1977.

Johan Elbers

Lazy Madge performed by Douglas Dunn and Jennifer Mascall of the Douglas Dunn Dance Company, 1976.

Nathaniel Tileston

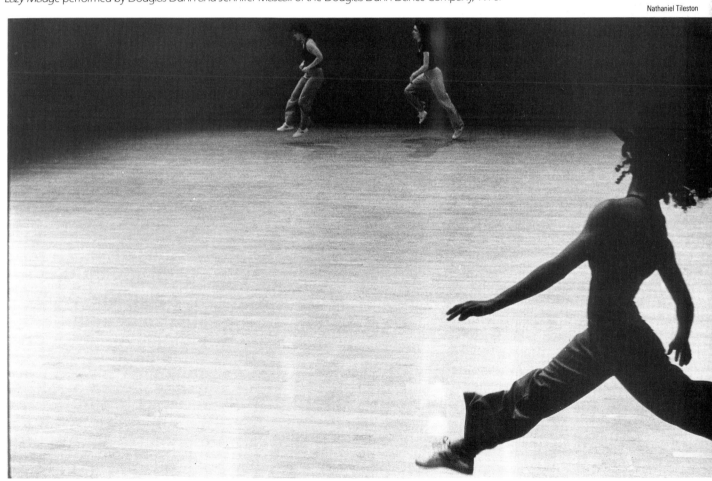

Sarah Rudner's *Dancing May's Dances* with Sarah Rudner, Wendy Rogers, and Francesca Bartocinni, 1976.

Lois Greenfield

Robert Wilson reinvents the theater in *A Letter to Victoria.*

Jennifer Muller and the Works in Muller's *White*, 1975.

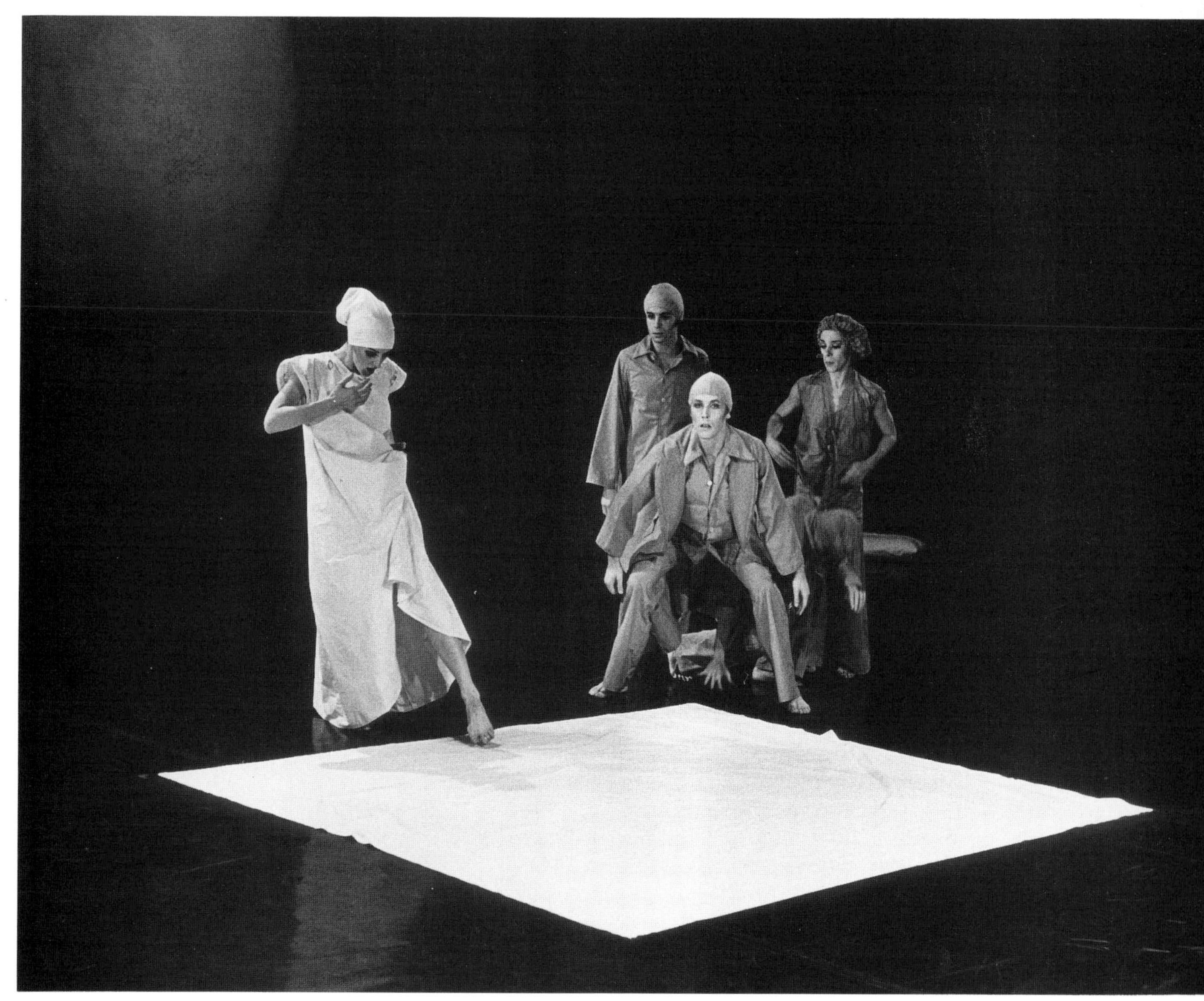

Johan Elbers

Nora Rotante in Ted Rotante's *Corporate Images II,* 1975.

Johan Elbers

Johan Elbers

Laura Dean and dancers in *Drumming,* 1975.

Gesture as Drama

The theater and cinema are trying to solve the problems of expressivity and technique in ways somewhat similar to the activities I have described in dance. Harold Pinter, for example, uses radical realism in a way similar to choreographers who deal with commonplace actions. He captures the absurdity of everyday conversation and rarifies it into a terrifying expression of an aimless human condition. This technique of dealing with the seemingly insignificant in a significant and entirely abstract way is reminiscent of Gertrude Stein's interest in words: their context, normal meaning, and purpose were ignored and they became valuable in terms of what they looked like and sounded like unto themselves. Despite her rejection of the objectivity which words usually convey in literature, the works of Stein are expressive. Exactly the same thing can be said of the concert dances of Merce Cunningham and Erick Hawkins.

Michelangelo Antonioni has discovered in his films an intriguing method of dealing with objective facts without using superficial "truth" (naïve realism) as the basis of his expressiveness. This method is particularly apparent in films like *Blow-Up* and *The Passenger*, in which he suspends plot and character development but evokes emotional reaction by borrowing various traditional techniques of melodrama to produce suspense, dread, excitement, etc., none of which however, are carried to their normal dramatic conclusion and none of which finally *mean* anything in terms of the films' content. Antonioni captivates his audience without telling us anything. He leads us into a metaphysical and ritual maze by luring us with emotional tensions which are in no way central or pertinent to his wholly abstract films. The end result is like the solo dance Alwin Nikolais created for Murray Louis in the second act of *Imago* — Louis' gestures evoke qualities like mystery, dread, and suspense without ever really dealing with them. Yet we don't feel in the slightest way cheated when the dance is over and these "feelings" turn out to have no real relevance to what the solo dance is really about. As Mark Schorer would say, *The content of a dance is only valid and meaningful to the extent that it has been used up by technique.*

Gesture, in art as in life, is always related to the human condition, no matter how metaphorically subtle and ritualistically reshaped it may be. This is true in dance whether the particular idiom is concerned with plot, characters, and dramatic gesture, or with pure, abstract gesture. Dance is gesture, and gesture is the rendering of a desired appearance without any actual representation of it, by producing the equivalent sense-impression rather than a literally similar one. When gesture serves dance in these ways dance becomes capable of rendering effects without actually imitating them; conveying a sense of motion and time without projecting events that connote anything in particular; and conveying a "dramatic" universe with objectified gestures instead of pantomime borrowed from actual situations. In dance, this process involves a transformation of the ideas furnished by reality into the materials from which the work of art is made.

Gesture is the manifestation of the total range of human movement. The only limitations of gesture in dance are the limits of human physiology. Each "school" of dance defines its perimeter of movement within the larger spectrum of possibilities. Someone like Erick Hawkins, for instance, would base his guidelines on his belief that just because a movement is possible does not make it desirable. Other choreographers, such as Yvonne Rainer, would stress utilitarian gestures, while

George Balanchine would embrace the mechanical vocabulary of the *danse d'école* as a point of departure.

Gesture is amplified bodily motion. By virtue of the kinesthetic basis of dance, the dancer's body is a highly developed neuromuscular resonator — like the resonance box of a violin — and it amplifies and projects its kinesthetic actions in an intensified form. The reproduction of a gesture by a dancer is like a musician

reenfield

The Concert Dance Company in *Pilobolus.*

sounding a tone on an instrument: it is a deliberate effect based upon a discipline which has been learned — and that applies equally to nondancers who learned as children the disciplines necessary to walk or to pick up an object, etc. Gesture is as explicit as tone. The interpretative quality of gesture is like the interpretative activity of a musician who is reproducing tone — the result of a purely qualitative function. For instance, the dancer possesses muscular "mutes" which alter the quality of movement and result in changes in the quality of visible gesture. The horn player knows that a specific kind of mute gives his intonation a distant, nostalgic sound. The *distance* as well as the *nostalgia* are not qualities of either the horn player or the note played. They are qualities of the mute. Exactly the same process — though it is infinitely more complex — is used by dancers in their control of the gestures they perform.

There is a vast potential spectrum for any gesture. At one end of the scale is the kind of expressiveness that has a discernible emotional quality. At the other end is the kind of control which permits a gesture to *achieve itself fully,* without any external references.

The Don Redlich Dance Company in *Slouching toward Bethlehem,* 1968.

courtesy Sheldon Soffer

Lois Greenfield

The Acme Dance Company in James Cunningham's *Apollo and Dionysus.*

Kenneth King and dancers in *Radio A.C.tiv(ID)ty,* 1976.

One of the major innovators in the theatre is Meredith Monk whose *Quarry* (1976) established new ground in the arts of the stage.

Nathaniel Tileston

Ritual as Art

We have been subdued. Our lack of the strength and stability of custom and the binding and sustaining power of communal tradition has subdued us. We have come to this difficult situation by a long and winding road, impelled by a trait which the Western world likes to call *typically human* but which is clearly nonexistent among a large part of the world's population — the drive to ceremonialize the unknown by means of specificity. It is this compulsion which turned the ambiguity of ritual into religious ceremony, and it is the same urgency to impose specificity upon everything we encounter that made us depose all power from our religious ceremonies and turn them into social customs. Now, the pursuit of specificity has been reshaped into the idealization of specialization,

Lois Green

James Cunningham and Barbara Ellmann of the Acme Dance Company in Cunningham's *Dancing with Maisie Paradocks*, 1973.

and this has brought us to our current technological predicament. Technique has replaced conviction. Artifice has replace ritual. We have arrived at the not very sublime summit, spinning our questionable motives into questionable prose, like the final lines of Curt Sachs' *World History of the Dance*: "This world is the living expression which has been the secret longing of man from the very beginning — the victory over gravity, over all that weighs down and oppresses, the change of body into spirit, the elevation of creature into creator, the merging with the infinite, the divine."

That Faustian proclamation perfectly summarizes the illusion which has brought us to the brink of extinction and divested us of most of our animal virtues along the way. We have become so "specifically" homo sapiens that we no longer relate to the animal world, which is, after all, our *only* world. But we think we are meant for the stars, and our technology is rapidly taking us there.

The victors of the Western world have won everything — and in the process have lost themselves. This loss is deeply felt by clans and cults which continually borrow from other people's ritual cultures. It is also felt by the people who work in art rather than in industry, and who do not particularly like the notion that humanity's crowning achievement will be technological self-extermination.

These artists are attempting to create rites of their own to compensate for the lack of rituals in their societies. Most of the great artists of our century — Joyce, Kafka, Bacon, Webern, Pollack — have built a *mysterious self* through their art to fill the vacuum left by the lack of public ceremonial life. And what, after all, is this mysterious ritual self? It is an appearance — an apparition, if you like. It springs from what we do but it is not what we are. It is something else. In watching a ritual we do not see what is physically before us. What we see is an interaction of forces by which something else arises. Those who only see what is before them are blind to all the other potentials of experience. Ritual, like art, requires us to really see. To see a virtual image, which is not unreal, for when we are confronted by it, it really does exist. The image in a mirror is such an image; so is a rainbow. It seems to stand on earth or in the clouds, but it really "stands" nowhere. It is only visible, not tangible. It is the unspeakable, the ineffable made momentarily visible, made experiential.

Contemporary artists are fascinated by technology, but they like to play with it rather than use it industriously. They use technology to produce apparitions, and this is heresy in terms of the Faustian dream. Artists are using the new technology to destroy technology, to reverse the process of *specificness* and specialization. They are using technology to produce that ambiguity which is at the core of ritual. Naturally this counterproductive urge of artists is nonsensical and repulsive to those striving for the stars. They want artists to be technical virtuosi. They want *real* art. They want *real* dancing — lots of fast, frantic, arduous dancing. They want to be uplifted — by rockets and supersonic aircraft. Somewhere over the rainbow, no doubt.

But what they need, and what dancing needs, is more rainbows.

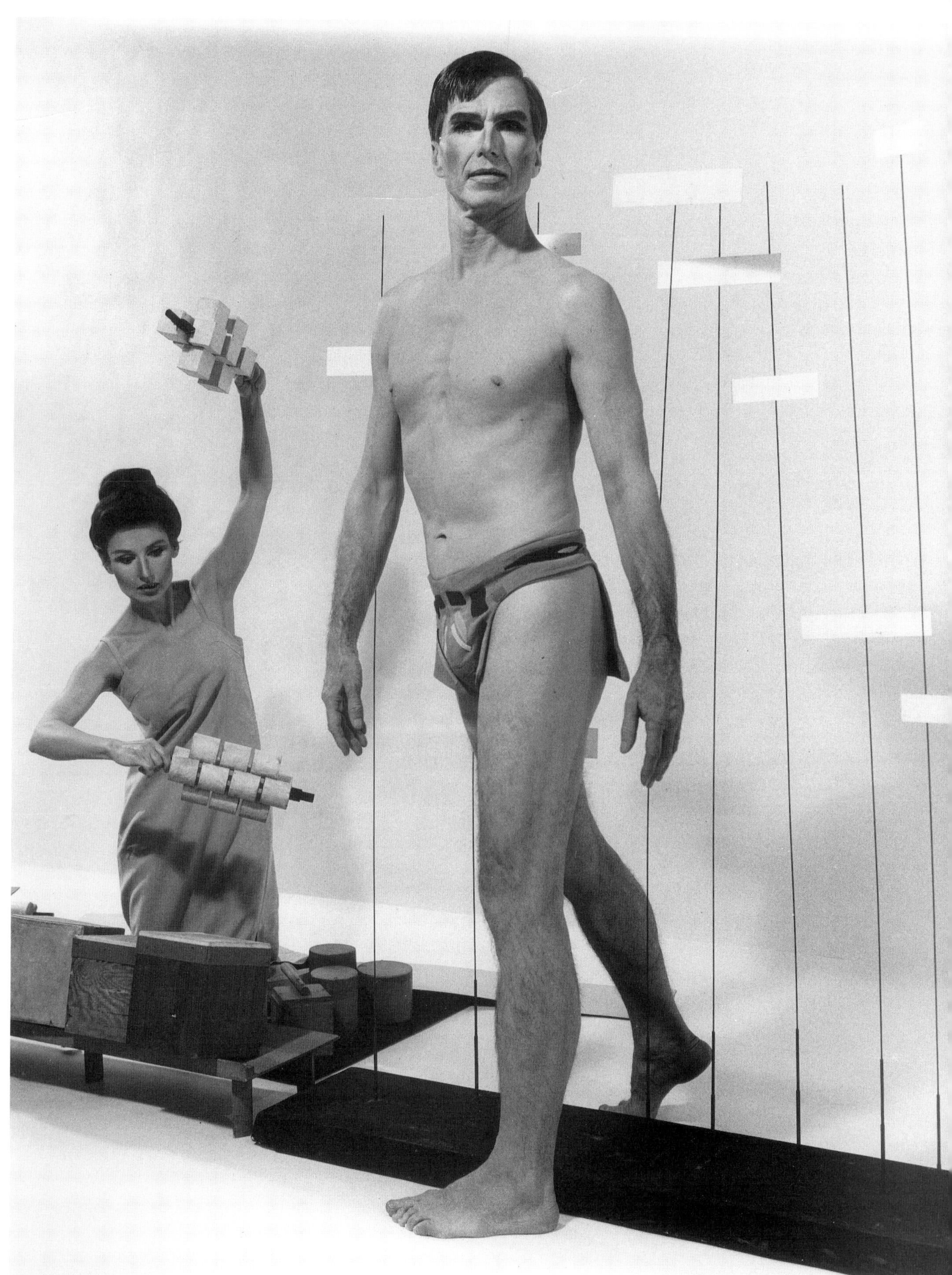

Erick Hawkins and Lucia Dlugoszewski in *Geography of Noon* by the Erick Hawkins Dance Company.

NOTES ON TWELVE CONTEMPORARY RITES

IT IS CONSIDERABLY easier to speak generally of dance than specifically. The critical standard used in the present often fails to comprehend the evolving art of the future. Just as artists must invent new techniques to deal with new vision, critics must develop new standards to deal with new art. During the interim, there is frequently a period of commentary which admits to being both tenuous and personal, insisting that new artistic experience requires nonconclusive, highly subjective responses rather than authoritative critical judgments.

The following notes on 12 dance works are such interim commentaries. They are impressions which range from brief notations to extended diatribes. Their length is not intended to express an evaluation of the comparative worth of the dances. In fact, the works I have selected are sometimes less important to me personally than some of those which I do not discuss. My choice of dances is based on the way they reflect the power of ritual or, contrarily, the way they lack substantial ritualistic impact.

JOSÉ LIMÓN: *THE MOOR'S PAVANE*

1 *The Moor's Pavane* has become a classic of modern dance. It is a special kind of dramatic, narrative dance, based on Shakespeare's *Othello* and on the compositional forms of the preclassic court dance called the *pavane.* The music is gathered from the suites for strings which Henry Purcell wrote as incidental music for various plays (one of which, ironically, is entitled *The Moor's Revenge*). The music used as accompaniment much predates the choreography, and there is, therefore, an anachronism at the core of *The Moor's Pavane.* The resolution of that anachronism was doubtlessly a vital source of creative imagination in the composition of this dance, as well as one of its major achievements.

All the thematic drama of this dance is interwoven into the steps and configurations of the pavane. The four characters (Othello, Iago, Desdemona, and Emilia) come from the circular pattern of the pavane. As they emerge from the circle, they adopt gestic character, which gives each of them individuality. When they return to the preclassic form of the pavane, they do so in terms of their character-

Milton Oleaga

Betty Jones and José Limón in *The Moor's Pavane.*

istic movement. It is the quality of movement and not the use of pantomime which imparts a sense of dramatic character in *The Moor's Pavane.* The external pattern of the dancing is a traditional preclassic dance. The pattern is only slightly developed from the original. The use of the circular form of the pavane provides a center of gravity, a configuration to which the dancers return periodically. The pavane lends a shape and regularity to the dance, dividing the narrative action into dramatically balanced segments. It also provides the basis for a merger of the seventeenth-century score with the Shakespearian story and the movements of modern dance.

Beyond the preclassic patterns of the pavane, Limón composed movement typical of his other dances, which deal with less archaic themes and which are danced to contemporary music. These "modern" movements, however, do not stand away from the preclassic matrix of the dance, for Limón has intriguingly blended various idioms. In all the movement, and especially that of the Moor (which Limón performed brilliantly), there is a Hispanic flavor which lends character and a fierce macho assertiveness.

The pavane at the center of this Limón dance provides more than an idiom for movement: it also serves the temporal patterns of the dance, lending a more or less rigid meter around which the freer rhythms of the dance revolve. There is little counterpoint in *The Moor's Pavane,* for the steps almost always imitate the music's beat and accent. Limón's choreographic relation to the music avoids monotony, however, by the careful selection of short musical segments from various Purcell suites which create contrasting moods and tempos. Interest is also created by the use of a variety of group arrangements: duets, solos, quartets, and trios. Because each of the four characters employs a different kinesthetic presence and, frequently, a different and characteristic body line, the movement of the quartet is invested with an individuality which greatly supports the dramatic progression as well as the compositional variety of the dance.

Limón devised a bodily manner for each of his four characters which provides dramatic tension. Iago employs a muscular attitude that is sinuous and grotesque. The Moor employs an open, heroic manner, while Desdemona is wistful and languid, her peripheral gestures unmarked by tension or the undulating muscularity of Iago and his wife.

The great dance photographer, Barbara Morgan, created this stunning protrait of José Limón in one of his early Indian works, *"Peon"* from *Mexican Suite,* 1944.

Barbara Morgan

These qualities lend a semblance of personality to abstract movement but are outside the imitative persuasions of the pantomimist's craft. Little gesture in *The Moor's Pavane* has a discursive relation to actual activity, and none of the movement attempts to refer to practical events of life. The dramatic thrust of the dance is infused into the structure of the pavane in the way that meaning is rendered in metaphor.

There *are* elements in *The Moor's Pavane* which are substantial rather than metaphoric. Desdemona's handkerchief, and all that it signifies in the Shakespearean drama, is inserted wholly and without much subtlety. This produces sequences of pantomimic action which obviously intend to communicate literal ideas, but tend instead to get in the way of the dance. The handkerchief is objectionable not because it is a prop but because it is used simply as a handkerchief, whereas dancers like Loie Fuller and Isadora Duncan integrated fabrics into the virtual forces of their dances. A scarf, for instance, was used as a kinesthetic extension of the body and not simply as a prop. More recently, Alwin Nikolais has developed a unique use of props as spatial protractions of human form and human motion.

The selective process by which Limón transformed narrative plot into a sequence of metaphoric actions is what makes *The Moor's Pavane* significant as dance. Clearly, the complex intrigue which surrounds the theft of Desdemona's handkerchief and Iago's presentation of it to Othello as an accusation of Desdemona's infidelity is an excessive, literal mouthful for dance. It is an element of the drama which was not successfully transformed into metaphoric action.

GEORGE BALANCHINE: *AGON*

2 In April 1957 Igor Stravinsky completed *Agon*, a work of great musical magnitude. In this score, he resumed the line of ballets he had created in a different stage of his musical career: *Apollo*, *Jeu de Cartes*, *Danses Concertantes*, and *Orpheus*. But with *Agon*, Stravinsky explored an entirely new musical idiom quite unlike anything he had previously composed for dance. Robert Craft, who often spoke for Stravinsky during his last days, said that the *Agon* pieces were "all modeled after examples in a French dance manual of the mid-seventeenth century." The title, Craft explained, was Stravinsky's own idea: "Stravinsky means the title to signify dance match or dance contest. 'Agon' is not a mythical subject piece to complete a trilogy with 'Apollo' and 'Orpheus.' In fact, it has no musical or choreographic subject beyond the new interpretation of the venerable dances which are its pretext. It was even conceived without provisions for decors and scenes — or, was independent at least in Stravinsky's mind of visual period and style."

Agon appears to be a very clearly shaped neo-classical dance.

Stravinsky's plan left nothing to the choreographer. The ballet was divided into three major sections: Part One, subsections A, B, and C; Part Two, subsections A through F; Part Three, subsections A, B, C, and D. He specified the nature and even the casting of each section and subsection. He called Part One, A, "Pas de Quatre." "Four male dancers advance to the rear of the stage with backs to the audience." And that's pretty much the way *Agon* begins. Part One, B calls for eight female dancers in the form of a double pas de quatre. Even more explicit instructions were given by Stravinsky for Part Two, B: "First 'Pas de Trois'; one male and two female dancers. 1) Sarabande step; male dance solo, two steps forward and three steps backward. 2) Galliard; two female dancers. 3) Coda; male and two female dancers." And for "Part Two, D": "Second 'Pas de Trois'; two male and one female dancer. 1) Bransle Simple; two male dancers. 2) Bransle Gay; female dance solo." Stravinsky's sketches indicate that the dancer must turn her head toward each of the male dancers in turn at the two points in the score where the instruments stop and the castanets play alone.

Stravinsky also gave the following instructions for Part Three, D, "Coda des Trois Quators": "Near the end, the female dancers leave the stage and the male dancers return to their original positions with their backs to the audience as at the beginning of the ballet."

There has never been a ballet score which attempted to do the choreographer's job to such an extent. It would seem that George Balanchine's only requirement in bringing *Agon* to the stage was providing fill for Stravinsky's thorough choreographic plan. The miracle, however, is that *Agon* turned out to be the superb dance it is. For all the splendid organization of Stravinsky's pretext, he said nothing in terms of what dance is essentially all about. The framework might have become a gigantic obstacle for Balanchine — trying to compose movement for an a priori plan. But Balanchine managed to supersede Stravinsky and to beat him at his own game. *Agon* is perhaps Balanchine's most inventive composition.

The composer capable of writing a ballet scenario is as rare as the composer equipped to write an opera libretto. The history of Stravinsky's ballets shows that he had little grasp of what makes ballets work as theatrical productions. Though Stravinsky made a habit of freely belittling his various choreographic collaborators for their lack of musical knowledge, he did not note his own lack of choreographic insight. For instance, it would have been easier to perform the steps of a sarabande to the music of a jazz band than to the music of Part Two, B, of *Agon* where Stravinsky nonetheless asked Balanchine to choreograph a sarabande. The virtue of the music for *Agon* is so great that Stravinsky's famous cantankerous manner with choreographers is unimportant, except as an indication of the challenge faced by Balanchine in composing this exquisite ballet.

George Balanchine works with seeming ease and apparent success in a great variety of choreographic modes. At his most avant-garde, his dances are curiously more modern than anything José Limón created. With *Agon*, Balanchine made one of his most daring and effective uses of abstract movement. His achievement tended to make modern dance works based on dramatic styles seem rather old-fashioned by comparison.

Agon is largely composed of sequences of disassociated movements. Balanchine has called *Agon* a "construction in space" and once compared it to an IBM computer. Traditionally, Balanchine relates the mode of his works to those qualities that are inherent in the music with which they are accompanied. He has a very special grasp of music, and his most inventive choreography seems to be the result of the imagination demanded of him by music. This is particularly true of *Agon*, which is far more inventive than Balanchine's choreography for a set of Charles Ives pieces he set under the title *Ivesiana*.

Agon is composed of numerous sets of variations on thematic gestures. Some sections make extensive use of canon form. Typical of many Balanchine ballets since 1955, there is an elimination of transitional steps, a manner which is very closely related to the rejection of traditional ideas about composition in the works of the most recent choreographers of modern dance. The familiar ebb and flow of movement, the tendency to produce steps "organically" so one emanates from another, the preparatory relaxation that usually precedes climactic steps — all these qualities are jettisoned by Balanchine. The dynamics of *Agon* are consistently intense. There is an absence of motive-consequence relationship. There is no effort to build choreographic anticipation or to satisfy it. In short, *Agon* is basically indistinguishable from some of the most challenging works of modern dance created fully two decades after Balanchine premiered the ballet.

From all this, it might be assumed that *Agon* makes abundant use of highly inventive steps, but the reverse is true. The interest of the ballet is not in its invention of steps, for Balanchine disclaimed any interest in discovering new movements. Working as he did in traditional ballet, he looked upon movement as an established vocabulary. What marks his work with imagination were his efforts to extend and invert familiar steps and combinations, manipulating the vocabulary to such an extent that it becomes almost unrecognizable. Steps may be executed with the knees turned in rather than turned out; the foot is often flexed rather than pointed (though this has proved to be a rather lame notion of modernism through repetition and abuse).

Every movement of *Agon* relates to balletic tradition, yet the movements are strangely new. Like the music of Stravinsky, the dance is eminently ordered and exceedingly clear in exposition, resting in a balanced, neoclassical framework which is neither staggering for its novelty nor impressive for its technicalities.

The climax of *Agon*, the section which shows the least signs of age, is the striking pas de deux (Part Two, F) where Balanchine achieves a really superb series of arduous variations.

There is no narrative or dramatic material in *Agon*. Even the sensual pas de deux is not remotely about anything and hasn't the least expression of a romantic encounter. Yet the ballet possesses a definite focus of interest, an evolving tension which moves through the alternation of quartets, octets, trios, sextets, and duets; which attains emphatic kinesthetic climaxes and decrescendos which convey a strong but indefinable network of feeling.

The groupings and spatial forms of *Agon* are not particularly novel. They are hardly more inventive than the group movements of Fokine's *Les Sylphides*. Symmetry is prevalent while asymmetric groupings are used to impart variety and tension. The movement is essentially hard-edged in character. The dancing is concerned with textures, rhythms, and shapes of motion. This kind of movement is divested of expression in its ordinary sense; it is not provoked by emotion or feelings about specific situations. The expressivity of *Agon* is bound to its move-

eorge Balanchine's *Agon*, performed by the New York City Ballet's
ana Adams and Arthur Mitchell in 1958.

L. D. Vartoogian

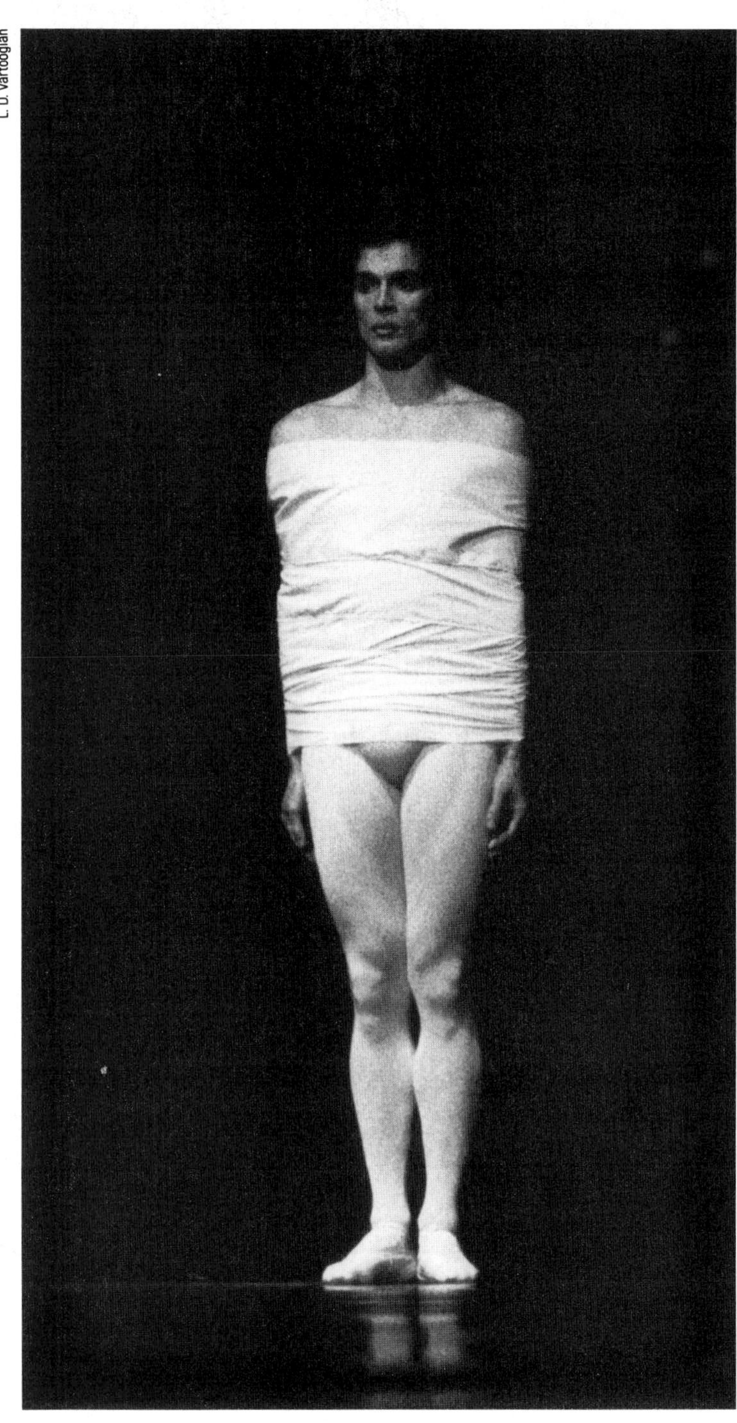

Rudolf Nureyev in the other great ballet by George Balanchine—*Apollo*—an early collaboration between Stravinsky and Balanchine.

ment. In accepting classical vocabulary as an ultimate value system, *Agon*, like the rituals which predate rationalism, does not need to be about anything but ballet itself. It is filled with the "meaning" which is implicit in the ideology of ballet and the sensibility which produced and perpetuated it. Yet *Agon* is not merely *the playful exercise of animal energy*, which people who defend pyrotechnical dance like to see in it. If it is "sport" then it is like the ancient, ritual games which were once played by the Maya and Aztec in the vast ball courts of Middle America. For on closer investigation the sports of our day are just as divested of their original expressive impulse as our most mindless dances. *Agon* renews the humanity of sport in what Stravinsky called "a dance contest."

3 The dance-drama *Circe* is not highly typical of the works of Martha Graham. Nonetheless, it achieves a special impact, which makes her ritual form particularly visible. *Circe*, unlike so many Graham dances, is not a memory play. It does not have the kind of recollective character which typifies many of Graham's dance-dramas and which gives motive to their mythic atmosphere. *Circe* is less pointedly intellectual than, say, *Clytemnestra*, *Cave of the Heart*, or *Night Journey*. In spatial style, *Circe* is far less constructionist than other Graham dances. It has wildly imaginative floor patterns. Frequently, and particularly at the climax of the dance, the figures run in a chaotic manner until they suddenly converge into a momentary symmetrical group, which accents its unison gestures with a strong rhythm.

The space of *Circe* is unlimited. The dance uses the upstage areas more than is usually the case in Graham's works. Circularity is a prominent pattern, but more often than not the spatial design of *Circe* is highly amorphous. The action of the dance takes place in the diagonal space between two set pieces: an upstage-right arch and a downstage-left arklike boat. These set pieces are not background decor but objects constantly involved in the movement. There

Martha Graham's *Frontier*, 1935.

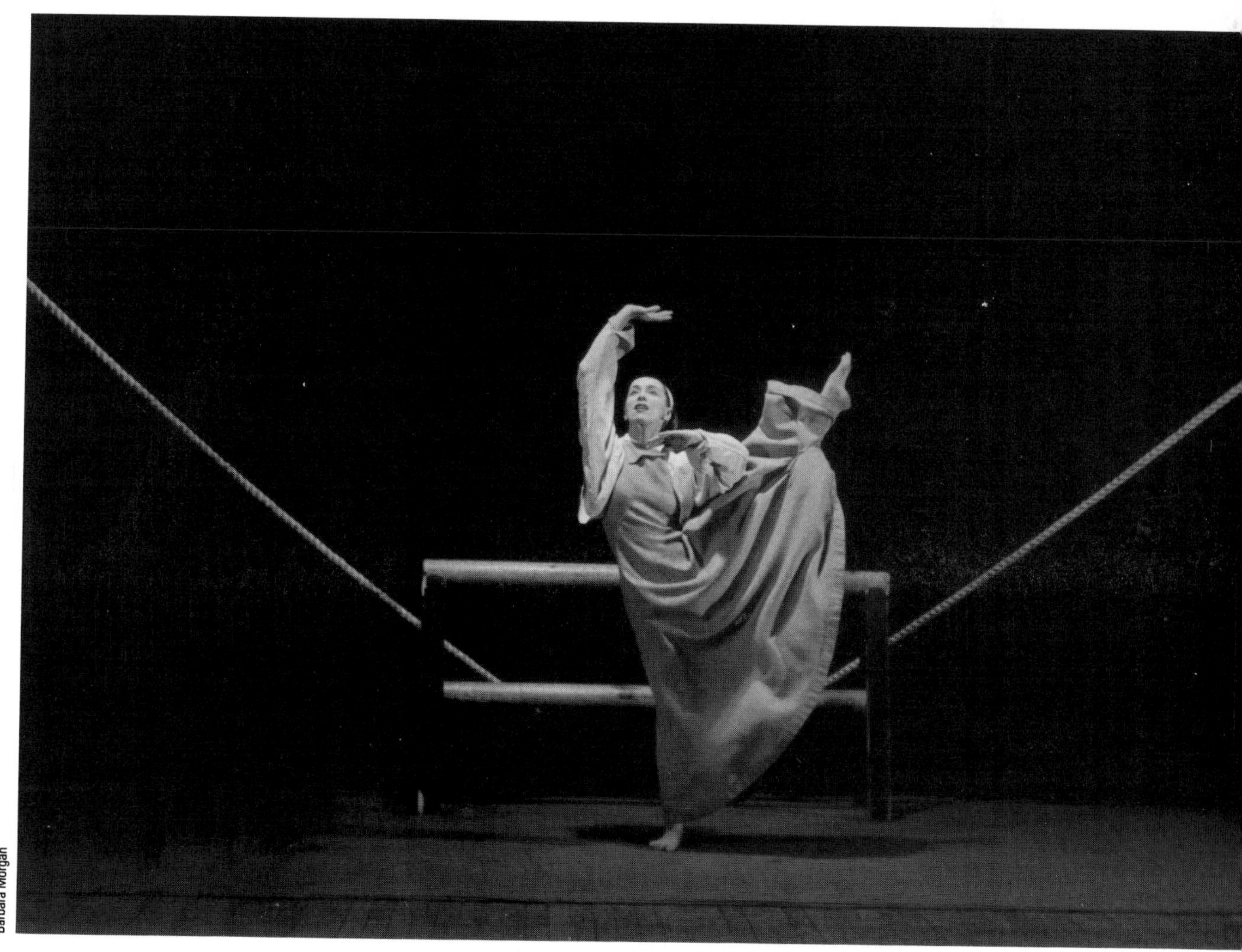

Barbara Morgan

seems little striving for an intellectual point in the involvement of the scenery with the dance movements; instead the relationship of the dancers and the scenic objects is utterly abstract and based on purely kinetic relationships.

Time is balanced between amazingly still sequences (Ulysses poised in frozen motion on the ark-boat) and passages of frantically detailed, percussive, exceedingly fast movements. In fact, there is so much movement in *Circe* that it is possibly the most densely choreographed of Graham's works. This means that its movement is exceptionally dense considering that, by the clock, Graham probably creates more movement in a dance per minute than any other contemporary choreographer.

The overall quality of movement in *Circe* suggests primal dance, especially tribal dances of Africa, a characteristic movement which seems to me unique in the works of Graham. Since *Circe* employs several male dancers, Graham has invented some of her most impressive movement for men, including some highly effective lifts and group gestures. The fact that Graham did not include herself in the cast of *Circe* may account at least in part for the unusual emphasis upon male dancers.

The theme of *Circe* calls for a highly charged erotic action. Graham, as always, is more than a bit old-fashioned and Freudian in suggesting a world in which sexual frustration is rampant and is a major driving power in all activities of life. The exchange between Ulysses and Circe is marked by considerable violence and frustration, an incomplete sexual exchange.

Sequentially, the dance-drama is quite simple: Ulysses and his crew land on an island. They are met by the bewitched and transformed figures of animal-men. Circe presents herself, uncoiling from concealment on the arch, and a pursuit ensues. Ulysses is saved from enchantment by his comrades and sails away. These actions are implicit, though they are conveyed without any use of pantomimic gesture or literalism. The plot of the dance-drama is simple enough and is exclusively concerned with unspecific dramatic action; therefore, the narrative evolution of *Circe* is accomplished without the need for discursive gestures.

What seems to interest Graham in *Circe* is the confrontation of Ulysses and Circe, as well as the animal aggression of Circe's captives, and the loyalty of Ulysses' comrades. Therefore, most of the dance is concerned with the meeting of the two major dramatic figures. This meeting is achieved entirely through abstract movement. There is no effort to convey events or characterizations. Graham works very fundamentally in this dance-drama and thereby succeeds in penetrating to the essential kinesthetic matrix of her dramatic theme. Gestures are at once gratifying as pure movement and dramatically effective and clear as metaphoric gesture. All the elements of the dance are ideally fused: music, setting, lighting, movement, and dramatic action.

It was probably Martha Graham more than any other single choreographer who discovered the basis for transforming plot into metaphoric action. Through her exploration of American Indian rituals and her interest in the mythologies of the ancient Western world, she evolved a highly personal style, at once theatrical and astonishingly ritualistic. Her idiosyncratic manner has been so great an influence on world theater and dance that it is still impossible to properly estimate her creative contribution to the arts of this century.

David Hatch Walker and Takako Asakawa in the Martha Graham Company's *Circe*.

y WNET/TV

Martha Graham and Erick Hawkins in *Puritan Love Duet* from *American Document*, 1938.

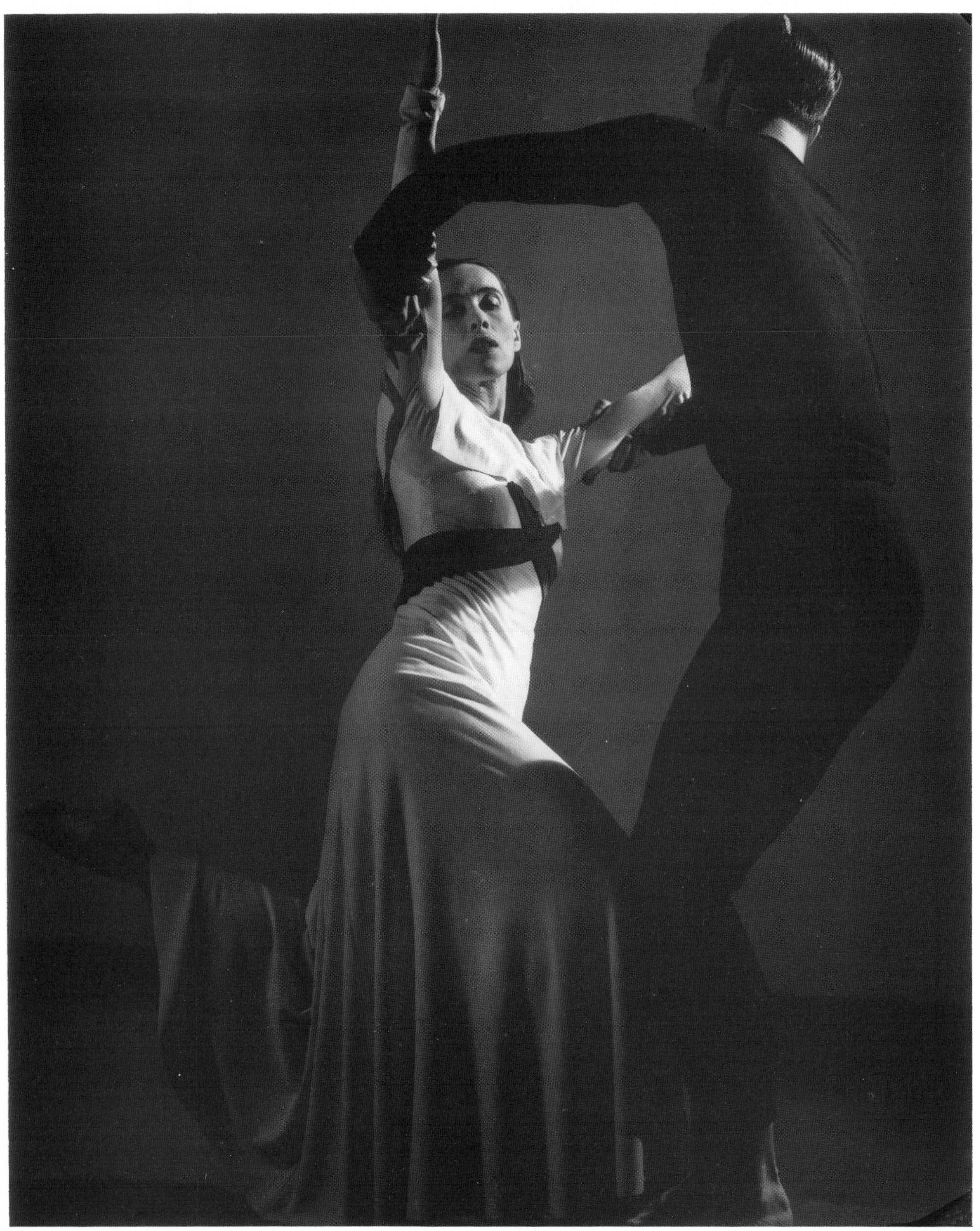

Barbara Morgan

ALWIN NIKOLAIS: *IMAGO*

4 *Imago* was created by Nikolais as a full evening work in 1963. His participation in the production was so central that it is impossible to speak of *Imago* as anything but a one-man show. Nikolais created the choreography, scenery, costumes, and lighting. He also collaborated with James Seawright on the score. The production, subtitled "The City Curious," is probably Nikolais' most influential work. It is also his most important composition. *Imago* typifies the idiom in which Alwin Nikolais has produced one of the three or four unique forms of dance in the post-Graham-Humphrey-Weidman era.

There is an obvious space-age atmosphere in *Imago* though the internal purposes of the dance appear to be concerned with matters far more fundamental than the depiction of a mechanistic-futuristic experience. The electronic score heightens the technological rather than the humanistic aura of the work, and the use of highly inventive costumes, props, and lighting also enhances the mechanistic atmosphere of *Imago*. Yet there is clearly at the base of the dance a distinctive, nonromantic core of expressiveness. Unquestionably, the words of Nikolais ritualize experience in terms of an entirely original vision. There are traces of the cosmos of the painters Léger and Dali; there is the influence of the fabric manipulation of Fuller and Graham; and there are even elements of Gordon Craig's "theater without people." Finally, however, the images of *Imago* and other Nikolais dances are unique.

It is often assumed that Nikolais wants to transform his dancers into humanoids, but I am convinced that something quite different motivates his marvelous metamorphosis of human beings and their world. Nikolais' ritual realm arises from a phantasmagorical imagination — and as such it contains every conceivable sensation of experience — microscopic, astronomic, and the world normally visible to us. What animates Nikolais' ontological rites is the amazement with which he infuses his images. *Imago* is not a slice of fictive life, like the film *2001*. Rather, it is a personal vision expressed through the communal devices of ritual, and implicit in the experience is Nikolais' role as Virgil, who conducts the spectator through all the realms which the contemporary imagination can summon. In other words, *Imago* is not impersonal science fiction; it is alive with the tensions and feelings which storytellers bring to shared adventures. There is both deep sentience and expressiveness in *Imago* but they are of a different resonance, a different focus, and a different momentum than our customary world of sound, sight, and motion.

The most immediate impact of Nikolais' dances comes in the excellent theatrical techniques he has invented, but his manipulation of stage space is only the beginning of his creative achievement, and it is a bit unfortunate that so many of his audiences get no further in their admiration for dances like *Imago*. Yet the purely technical aspects of his works are admittedly as astonishing as his expressive power. Nikolais manipulates space in an entirely new manner. Through the use of wires, costumes which extend the dancers' limbs, lighting projections, and other theatrical devices, Nikolais succeeds in altering the stage space and in reaching an area rarely touched by performers: the space above the dancers' heads. This space, the region between the proscenium and the performers, is never used in dance. Normally, it is "filled" by the static design of a backdrop. Nikolais, however, ascends into that untouched area and manages to employ the *whole canvas* of stage space. In one segment of *Imago* he has arranged wires and pendantlike shapes in such a manner that the action of two dancers manipulates the motion of the pendants and creates an astonishing interplay with their own bodies. In yet another sequence of the production, the dancers are equipped with dehumanizing costumes which provide their arms with wondrously extrahuman form, size, and length. At one point, these figures stand one behind the other, facing the audience, and through the use of serial (rather than unison) gesture, they create an extraordinary spatial protraction, which the human body is normally incapable of. Yet the resulting movement is impressive not because it is beyond our kinesthetic grasp but for precisely the opposite reason: it extends our bodily imagination beyond the range of our normal potential for movement and amazes and intrigues us, and fills us with a sensation of frightful exuberance which is unique to Nikolais' theater.

Imago is not concerned with human conduct, but it is nonetheless highly humanistic in its impact. To an unusual extent, Nikolais has succeeded in

The Alwin Nikolais Dance theatre in *Cross Fade,* 1974, another Nikolais work of later vintage.

courtesy Nikolais Dance

Milton Oleaga

Alwin Nikolais Dance Theatre in *Imago,* 1963.

alienating human action from human motivation, envisioning an entirely credible, but unreal, reality. As such, *Imago* seems to affirm the beauty and sentience intrinsically involved in the most sublime and creative aspects of science, those which confirm rather than deny the worlds produced by imagination.

In matters of gesture, Nikolais is essentially concerned with nondiffusive, nondramatic movements which are highly expressive in terms of muscular tension and temporal repetition. Undulation is almost nonexistent in *Imago*. Transition is achieved as a matter of precise changes in the anatomical relationship of a hard, defined space. There is considerable inner tension in the gestures of *Imago*; a kind of resistant tension like elasticity without resilience. This type of motion was perfectly performed by dancers Murray Louis and Phyllis Lamhut in the 1963 premiere. As such the movement is like a foreign language which we do not understand but which conveys to us something more fundamental than the connotation of words.

Imago is an experience almost indistinct from that of a rainbow: it represents before us things which are not tangible but are capable, as virtual images, to make their momentary appearance. These images live in a dense atmosphere of colored light, penetrating deeply into a space unfamiliar to our bodies. They perfectly combine the familiar with that which is utterly strange. The impact is ultimately unique, for it pronounces in sight and sound a nonaesthetic scientific thesis in the form of art.

5

The usual intention of dancing — and that includes abstract dance despite its claims of ambiguity — is to depict what is before us and what is happening to us. There was a time when painting had much the same purpose. About the time of Cézanne, though, it must have occurred to somebody that the process didn't work if artists were really trying to stir responses in their audience. They learned that accurately rendering an experience did not guarantee that those people seeing the rendition would feel what the artist had felt. So painters began to put aside the "naïve realistic" aim, and instead of painting what evoked strong sentience in them, they began to paint the sentience itself. Gradually, the object of the picture disappeared into its expressiveness. The technique was entirely used up by the subject and the subject was entirely used up by the technique.

It seems to me that this process is central in our era both in the arts generally and in dances of Merce Cunningham in particular.

The process I have described is a well-known sequence in the development of nonrealistic art. Since its inception, it has taken countless turns, but what is still at the heart of any discussion of media is the method by which an artist, writer, composer, or choreographer evokes response, no matter what kind of response is evoked or how well it is done. That this central theme of twentieth-century art expression has entered so rarely, so meekly, and so ineffectually into dancing is what makes the dances of Merce Cunningham so valuable. Cunningham is trying to get psychology and literalism out of dancing by refusing to accept the traditional responsibility of choreographers to depict "realistically" what is before them and what is happening to them.

We all know that there is an enormous, inexpressible gap between what we feel and the methods at our command for depicting our experiences. This situation is especially apparent if we are choreographers who use movement for more than matter-of-fact existence. The results of this predicament are complicated, but some of them are relevant to the methods used by Cunningham. The more he is confronted as a choreographer with the nearly unbearable materiality of movement, the more he grasps that the very emotional context of movement which allows him to communicate also automatically limits and defines what he is able to convey to an audience. Cunningham has reacted to this conclusiveness of movement by becoming intrigued by the process of making motions as a thing unto itself. He looks for shortcuts which can lead directly from what is experienced to the stage itself. For this reason, most of the dances of Merce Cunningham are not only produced without plots and characters but also, in a special sense, without a choreographer.

What we see in Cunningham's *Rainforest* are emblematic forms built out of the medium of motion without the intrusion of the process by which movement normally communicates, therefore shaping and limiting the so-called bounds of dance. We also see a good many examples of irony, which Cunningham uses to produce new forms by ridiculing the methodology of old choreographic forms. Some of his dances are fairly straightforward, while others take their lead from the dadaists of 1916–1920. The most interesting pieces are those which create an activity which views the very space of the stage (or any other space) as an emblem-

Valda Setterfield and Bryan Mehl in the Merce Cunningham Dance Company's production of *Rainforest,* with decor by Andy Warhol and music by David Tudor.

ty; courtesy Cunningham Dance Foundation

atic theater where motion, image, succession, and form have a life of their own. Cunningham makes it clear that he can assert new ideas of what dancing is all about, and in doing this, he is producing effects with movement, lighting, props, and costumes which imply an entirely original method for turning experience into ritual.

Cunningham also uses randomness and indeterminacy as positive forces for constructing dances in an era in which all rationale for artistic form has been destroyed by the decline of universal values in society and art. In a time when few of us are committed to anything, Cunningham is so totally committed to the New York art scene that he permits it to march through his dances like celebrities on a promotional tour. When *Rainforest* is performed, the Mylar plastic pillows of Andy Warhol are on hand; so is the music of David Tudor. If they are the kinds of things you like, then you can take notice of them for awhile. There is no particular reason for them to be there, but there is also no reason they shouldn't be part of *Rainforest*.

This informal attitude toward what is and what is not important in a dance is the basis of Cunningham's innovative power. Behind the vigorous randomness of Cunningham's stagecraft is choreography which is so fundamental to Western theatrical dancing that it might as well be ballet. In fact, most of Cunningham's dancers are so highly trained in ballet that their movement is sharply at odds with the choreographer's own execution of his steps.

Cunningham's movement, whether for himself or his company, has extremely clear lines and tends to work outward from an upright though unrigid spine. There

Another Cunningham opus — the Merce Cunningham Company in *Travelogue*.

J. L. Vartoogian

Lois Greenfield

The Merce Cunningham Company in Travelogue.

is great speed in the movement and a tendency to shift weight and directions with a rapidity uncharacteristic of the modern dance which preceded his works. *Rainforest*, like all his dances, makes use of the actions of everyday life — walking, running, etc. Cunningham is totally removed from the theatrical idealizations of Martha Graham, who believes that movement has explicit emotional significance and that dancing is an expression which is loftier than the commonplace. Cunningham rejects as artificial all the principles of "theatrical nobility" which dominated the ideas of dance and drama for centuries. Yet, in rejecting as nonsense the Graham notion that all movement means something, Cunningham does not presume that his dances are abstract and devoid of expression. Emotion, he says, is always present in dancing "because it's a human being doing it. A human being is not an abstract. I never considered my dancing abstract. Everyone else did, but I don't. I think that everything a human being does is expressive in some way of that person." The feeling of a movement "will appear when that movement is danced, because that's where the life is. The life does not lie outside the dancing, however strange or nonstrange, conventional or nonconventional the dancing is, the life of a dance lies there."

Cunningham introduced an idea to modern dance which is also central to George Balanchine's ballets: making dances about nothing but dancing itself. Technically, there is a good deal of common ground between Cunningham and Balanchine. Cunningham, however, made the breakthrough which sent many young dancers into a whole new era of choreographic sensibility. That influence is founded upon the *context* of Cunningham's dances far more than his inventions of original movement. In other words, the impact of his dances is founded upon conventional climaxes which arise from an assortment of curiously appealing, unconventional and random elements, each of which is largely going its own way. All the brilliant peculiarity of the stage is an optional backdrop for dances which move with force and persuasion to the most ordinary theatrical climaxes — the dancers picking up a strong beat and, one at a time, rhythmically whirling off stage like flamenco dancers making one of those frantically theatrical exits. Or, in *Rainforest*, a woman performing a regal, energetic solo, which attracts one of the three men in the dance who joins her in a duet of great assertiveness before the woman leaves and the man follows after her. Thus the stage is abandoned in the most theatrical manner, leaving behind an emptiness except for a nodding crowd of silver pillows as the curtain falls.

The Merce Cunningham Company in *Travelogue*.

Lois Greenfield

ERICK HAWKINS: *BLACK LAKE*

6 Erick Hawkins reawakens in us our heritage as animals. He helps us to recall the impulse for motion within us which is animal. Yet, he is not interested in the current vogue for naturalness. His world of movement is *essential* rather than natural. When Hawkins dances, we see movement which comes from the condition of having an animal's body. It is like watching lions, turtles, and eagles, which characterize every detail of their activities with the unique physical fact that they are lions, turtles, and eagles.

I don't think we have ever really known, as other animals seem to know, what it is to have the specific kind of bodies we have or exactly how we are supposed to use them. We have had a great many elaborate substitutes for who we are and what kind of animal bodies we have. We have constructed some outrageous illusions about our specialness among other creatures. And no one easily sees the human animal hiding under its many disguises.

Erick Hawkins sees the creature within us. He is able to remember our infancy among the other animals. In his dances that memory becomes clear to us. We recognize the essential human body within us just as we recognize lions in the motion of lions.

To find an animal body within himself Hawkins had to abandon the narrative dancing he performed in the early days with the Martha Graham company. That kind of dancing was so intent upon the human psyche that it very nearly ignored the human body. Merce Cunningham also left Graham to get away from psychology. Both Hawkins and Cunningham went in search of a new principle of movement by going back to basics. Cunningham is stupendously rational, and so he became convinced that classicism was the fundamental stuff from which everything evolves. Hawkins is impelled by something more primary. He wanted a physical, not a logical, reason for dancing. And he knew that he could find it in the body which exists within our bodies — the spiritual body.

As a result of this discovery, Hawkins has evolved a complex premise of human movement from which everything most distinctive in his choreography flows. It is a principle so basic that it lies beyond and beneath matters of style and individuality in dancing. Hawkins has used that principle to create dances which are unique in their reflection of his underlying technique and in their expression of his immense individuality as a choreographer.

Black Lake is an ideal example of Hawkins' recollection of our animal heritage. It sees the land and the creatures of the land with eyes which have not turned upon the world before. It makes us feel that we have never seen the sun, stars, or moon before. With the renewal of our animal impulse we also regain the real world which produced us. *Black Lake* celebrates that world, and it becomes part of the future because it draws new vitality from the most distant memories of the past.

The eight sections of *Black Lake* are ritual actions of such essential vision that they are indistinct from the most mysterious of Pueblo dances. The rite begins with a masked figure placing a mask on the face of a female figure in a ceremony which reminds me of the secretive preparations of the masked kachinas in Pueblo rituals. Once the mask has touched the face of the female, she is instantly

Erick Hawkins in *Summer Thunder* from *Black Lake*.

Cathy Ward in the Erick Hawkins Dance Company's performance of *Comet* from *Black Lake*.

David Fullard

Erick Hawkins and Robert Yohn in the Erick Hawkins Dance Company's *Night Birds* from *Black Lake*.

transformed into a human animal, so viable and mutable that it can produce the apparitions of the smallest and the greatest things in nature: the sun, the fire star, night birds, the moon with clouds, and the comet. With the rich simplicity of Ralph Dorazio's paper costumes, the masked dancers can perform serene and startling transformations. And behind and ahead of these ageless processions of human animals is the music of Lucia Dlugoszewski, rising out of the uniqueness of the human ear just as Erick Hawkins' movements arise from the singularity of our animal bodies.

Black Lake ends with the first masked male untying the mask of the female dancer. Then, one at a time, all the others remove their masks. What is revealed behind the masks is the most mysterious revelation of all — the human face — so astoundingly new that we do not recall ever seeing it. It is like the close of the initiation rites of Pueblo Indians when the kachinas remove their masks in the presence of the young initiates, who discover for the first time that the kachinas are only human, but human animals filled with great power.

Erick Hawkins awakens us to the wisdom of Black Elk who once said: "The giving earth remembers and only men forget. The animals and man have lost their little dreams and have awakened together." In Erick Hawkins, a bit of the dream is recovered.

ROBERT WILSON: *EINSTEIN ON THE BEACH*

7 The opera by Robert Wilson and Philip Glass, *Einstein on the Beach*, is a ceremony in which Albert Einstein becomes a kachina (or, rather, a group of kachinas). Wilson made no attempt to describe Einstein in biographical terms. He transformed everything he and his associates felt, knew, and guessed about Einstein into a series of kachina rites. These rites reflect the catastrophic images of Fritz Lang's *Metropolis* and Nevil Shute's *On the Beach*, as well as the composite images of Charlie Chaplin and Adolph Hitler fighting out a battle of survival in the face of both the awesomeness and futility of science and the curiosities of time and space.

Watching *Einstein on the Beach* was like watching paint dry. The fundamental structure of ritual used up all the complex ideals of Wilson and Glass, reshaping everything into nine long rites of initiation, in each of which a single microcosmic act was so eloquently slowed down that we were given the unusual opportunity of witnessing the primal power that lies behind the reality which most people accept as absolute. Philip Glass evolved his one-note composition into a strange music of enormous persuasion and power, making exquisitely refined use of amplification, vocal utterance, and the sort of sequential tone dominant among primal peoples but unknown in much of Western civilization. The Glass score is structurally astonishing, while at the same time completely obvious and theatrical, possessing a tension and momentum which succeeds in reuniting music and action in its ancient ritualistic form.

Like the famous *Monkey Chant* of Bali, the music by Glass for *Einstein on the Beach* moves equally in time and space. It is extremely easy music, in contrast to the harmonic difficulties which many listeners find in the works of major composers of the first half of the century. This minimalism in the development of musical line and the use, instead, of very gradually evolving rhythmical tensions makes the score ideal for the unique idiom of dance-theater for which Robert

Babette Mangolte

Robert Wilson's *Einstein on the Beach.*

Wilson has become renowned. His is a theater of methodical, simple sequences with a deep sense of the succession which was at the core of the works of Gertrude Stein. Very little "happens" in *Einstein on the Beach*. And when something does happen, it is likely to be a single, short action that is repeated again and again until a very special quality of feeling and meaning arises out of the repetition. This process reminds me of the word lists which Stein composed: their endless winding without apparent syntax eventually evoked a semblance of meaning, which relied little on the normal context and definitions of the words themselves. Rather, something quite beyond the specific evolves out of the experience of both Stein's prose and Wilson's stagecraft.

Lucinda Childs is a marvelous, moving figure who interweaves all the elaborate diversity of *Einstein on the Beach* into an integrated experience. I do not think I have ever been more moved by a single moment in the theater than by the haunting redundancy of Childs ceaselessly prancing forward and back, forward and back, while the stage is transformed by Wilson's magic realism — a steel tower, a margin of white neon light, and a huge pasteboard steam locomotive edging falteringly across the horizon.

Like all genuine rituals, *Einstein on the Beach* answers all questions asked of it by showing us how ridiculous questions are. In the office of the *Einstein* company in Avignon, France, there is a Chekhov quotation pinned to the wall: "The illusions which exalt us are dearer than a thousand sober truths." *Einstein on the Beach* perfectly refutes that romantic platitude. Robert Wilson and Philip Glass show us that not all myths are illusions and not all myths exalt us.

8

There are worlds of difference between the music and choreography of Laura Dean and that of the dancers and musicians of Bali. The difference between the works created by the Balinese and *Spiral*, composed and choreographed by Laura Dean, is one of fundamentality versus superficiality. The fundamentalism of the music of composers like Terry Riley or the thoroughly assimilated and creative "orientalism" of composers like Alan Hovaness and Philip Glass seem beyond the reach of Laura Dean. What should be heightened sensuality in the repeated motives of the music turns out to be deadly redundancies. What should be polyphony and massive layers of sound turns out to be a 32-bar pop backing track. What wants to give impressions of profundity and fundamentality turns out to be superficiality in long durations.

The Balinese know better. Their orchestra is the total of its numerous instruments, individually played but producing a unified contrapuntal impact. Each player plays only one melody at a time. In the largest, most resonant instruments the melody is simply a phrase, slow and short and repeated again and again like an endless sound. The smaller and higher-pitched instruments play in unison melodies of exceedingly subtle and swift complexities. The combination of all of these melodies (which the Western ear does not hear as melodies but as modulat-

Lois Greenfield

cers of Bali.

Erin Mathiessen, Angela Caponigro, and Laura Dean (at piano) of the Laura Dean Dance Company in Dean's *Song*.

courtesy Japan Information Service

From traditional Kabuki dance-drama to contemporary Japanese-American modern dance — a scene from *Funa-Kenkei*, a Kabuki drama.

ing rhythms) produces a unique polyphony as well as a series of massive layers of sound. The fundamentality of Balinese music lies in the intricate variations on the main themes and in the rhythmic complexities introduced by the stage-left drummer who is the leader of the orchestra and whose intricate gestures are a kind of choreographic form of "conducting." This Balinese music is a superstructure of redundant 4/4 beats surrounding a creative core of exquisite syncopations and added beats, the improvised expression of the individual drummer. In Balinese music there is an outer composition, but there is also an inner pulsation, an inner core of the music's percussive and chordal life. What is lacking in the music of Steve Reich, to a very great extent, and lacking from the musical conception of Laura Dean is that essential inner core.

Dean's choreographic ideas suffer from the same superficiality as her musical efforts. Her dance work, *Spiral*, strives for a realm of incantation and ritual which is entirely out of its reach. By contrast, Asian dance possesses an immediate access to a control, a sense of detail, and an implicit expressiveness

Kei Takei in *Light Part 10,* 1976.

Johan Elbers

which is the essence of ritualism. Laura Dean borrows elements from cultures which are exotic and alien to her: she uses the mystical dervish of the temple of Mevlana in Konya like a naïve kid from Staten Island producing tireless, technological spinning rather than a subtle outpouring of power from the core of the inner spindle of life. She uses the mudras of India but fails to use the awareness which is intrinsic to the Hindu's grasp of dance as an activity of the *spiritual body*. Laura Dean's dancers perform long and hard — and they arouse applause, but their achievement is technological and not spiritual, which is what Dean is supposed to be all about. In her music and in her dance, Dean has a complex lesson to learn from the Orient from which she borrows so much and so little. There is an inner and an outer dance — an inner and outer core of music, too. When we are content with the outer shape of things and present them candidly and repeatedly as profound truth, we are likely to be dealing with superficiality but calling it fundamentality. Primal peoples have understood this pitfall for centuries — civilizations are just learning about it.

9

Bebe Miller is a strong new force in dance. Performances of her young company offered some of the most fascinating works of the 1980s postmodern movement. Bebe Miller's choreography is original and innovative at the same time that it embraces all that is best and nothing that is bromidic about postmodernism. For instance, in the hour-long opus *Allies*, her company of three women and three men is completely unrestricted by stereotypes of gender — a welcome trend that has become a powerful element of postmodern dance. Women are not aggrandized as helpless and fragile nymphs, to be lifted and carried across the stage by their sturdy cavaliers. To the contrary, women lift male dancers and female performers lift and carry other females, far more often than the men lift the women. Such revisioning of cultural and sexual attitudes in dance conveys a subtle and ambiguous sensuousness rarely witnessed in older forms of Western dancing, in which the gender roles of men and women were highly standardized.

There are also many all-male duets and trios, including lyrical lifts and "adagios," that are executed with deeply touching effect. Though *Allies* has no explicit program or pretext and does not strive for literal meaning, these changes in the physical relationships of the performers convey several important messages about human kinships. In this way, Miller's unisexuality provides depth and substance to her theme in *Allies*, which, at least on one level, is concerned with the joys and sorrows of many different kinds of human relationships.

Miller's choreography possesses the nonchalance and relaxation that is characteristic of most postmodern dances; dancers reel and leap with a streetwise naturalness; individuals are not submerged in a strict sameness of style and appearance; toes are not fully pointed; and there are few efforts to achieve a pyrotechnic effect.

Yet *Allies* manages to sustain, for more than an hour, a persistently innovative movement vocabulary, evolving numerous surprises out of familiar forms that are engaging in their lyricism, effective in their theatrical aggression, and often deeply touching in their allusion to human feeling.

Like most postmodern choreographers, Bebe Miller has catholic sensibilities that absorb many different influences and lifestyles. For instance, the *Allies* music by Fred Frith straddles that old barrier that used to be raised between so-called classical and popular music. The rhythms are often pop; while the harmonic development is lavishly classical in its complexity.

Miller adds large episodes of silence to Frith's commanding score, and she manages to use both the music and the silence to great purpose, sometimes operating entirely in counterpoint to the music; while at other times producing a powerful ensemble sequence to the primal thump of the beat.

Allies is every bit as strong in its spatial ideas as it is in its varied movements. Miller achieves an added dimension of meaning and emotion by her use of the isolated space behind two transparent scrim-structures designed for the stage by Robert Flynt. The figurative paintings on those scrims were distracting, but the structures themselves, which many choreographers would treat simply as pictorial backdrops, were put to vivid use. This spatial awareness was aided by

The rhythm of a jump by Bebe M

the lighting design of Ken Tabachnick, which heightened the theatrical fullness of *Allies* by underscoring its spatial forms and its emotional language.

There are some youthful flaws in Bebe Miller's ritual approach to dance. In the words of novelist and diarist Anaïs Nin, the process of ritualization in the arts is an effort "to create a world that is truer than the one that stands before us." Miller is inclined to overstate realistic details that seem to have little place in the broad and metaphoric scope of her choreography. This inclination is especially visible in the opening five or ten minutes of *Allies*, which is performed in silence. The unfortunate naturalism of the dancer's dramatic gestures verges on bad acting; they seem intent upon "telling" us something we don't need to know.

Though Bebe Miller herself is a black artist from New York City, she had no black dancers among the ranks of the company that I saw. She has said that her work is about being a human being, not about being African-American. She wants her creative work to be *colorless*, which, she reminds us, is what the real struggle for racial equality is all about.

The dancers performed with great skill and commitment, producing the kind of joy that will surely carry the Bebe Miller Dance Company triumphantly throughout the 1990s.

GARTH FAGAN: *PRELUDE* AND *OATKA TRAIL*

10

Garth Fagan's career in dance began when he left his native Jamaica as a teenager to tour Latin America with Ivy Baxter and the Jamaican National Dance Company. Later, in New York City, he studied with Martha Graham, José Limón, Mary Hinkson, and Alvin Ailey. Then, in 1970 as a professor at the State University of New York at Brockport, Mr. Fagan began teaching a handful of untrained dancers at the university's inner-city center in Rochester.

Some of those early students still remain at the core of Garth Fagan Dance, an ensemble with rare congruity of style and technique, with profound expressiveness and unlimited energy.

Garth Fagan Dance, which is based in Rochester, New York, does not look like any other dance company. The Fagan technique that underscores every aspect of the company's performances is so complex that it is difficult to describe Fagan's choreographic individuality. But *individual* it is!

On first impression, the 1981 ensemble piece *Prelude: Discipline Is Freedom* was strongly "racial," with driving African-American energy, full-bodied movement, and highly rhythmical accompaniment. That impression, however, soon falls short of what Fagan is really all about. As he has said, "I'm interested in ethnicity and not in race." It is culture, not folklore, that stimulates his imagination.

So, despite the unquestionable influences from such noted Caribbean dancers as Pearl Primus and Lavinia Williams, ultimately Garth Fagan Dance has almost no relationship to those Afro-American dance companies. Fagan has created something infinitely more complex and visionary than the highly theatrical work of black choreographers like Katherine Dunham and Alvin Ailey. This daring invention becomes unmistakable a few minutes into *Prelude*

— which is doubtlessly called a prelude essentially because it was designed as a rousing opening work for Fagan programs. After its initial impact, what gradually overwhelms the energy and frenzy of the dancing is a choreographic sensibility of remarkable subtlety and sophistication and clarity.

Few choreographers use space as imaginatively as Garth Fagan does. His stage is a vast canvas that is persistently and inventively shaped and reshaped by brilliantly conceived entrances and exits, by constantly changing groupings, by the unexpected interactions of solos, duets, trios, and quartets. Even at its most rhythmical moments, when the audience shouts and applauds with kinesthetic pleasure, even then Fagan manages to elicit a highly theatrical response with his rarefied choreographic imagination. The leaping, bounding, undulating, and darting figures are transformed almost magically. A driving trio shatters into three frantic solos, until a fourth dancer ricochets across the stage and the four soloists collide and become an elegant quartet, which mysteriously comes apart and turns into four streaks of light, flying off into infinity.

The Garth Fagan Dance Company in *Sojourn*.

Steve Labuzetta, courtesy Garth Fagan Dance

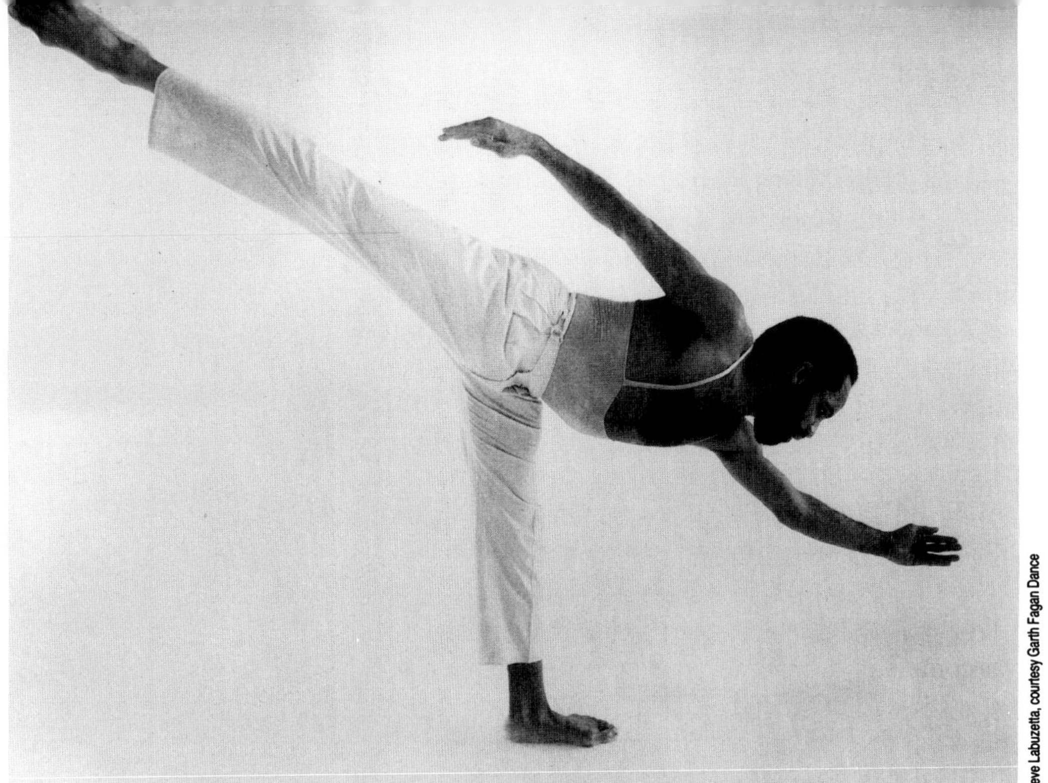

Steve Labuzetta, courtesy Garth Fagan Dance

A. Roger Smith in Garth Fagan's *Oatka Trail,* inspired by an old Seneca Indian trail near Rochester, New York.

The frenetic atmosphere of *Prelude* is nowhere to be found in the lyrical 1979 opus, *Oatka Trail,* performed to the slow movement of a cello concerto of Antonin Dvořák. This male trio reveals the innermost nature of Fagan's lyricism. It is a rare sensibility, without a hint of either sentimentality or prettiness. In *Oatka Trail* bodily grace has retained its animal dignity. It has not become romantic artifice. *Oatka Trail* also underscores Fagan's exceptional musicality, which never allows him simply to supplement the emotional impact of the music or merely to articulate the obvious cadences.

Garth Fagan's choreography is a response to the music, not an imitation of it. It often interacts with both the musical line and the rhythm, but on the whole Fagan prefers to create contrapuntal movements and sequences with their own line and rhythm. The result can be emotionally shattering, as, for instance, at the closing decrescendo of the Dvořák, when the three figures alternatively glide and frantically step and gesture in utter harmony as well as complete contrast to the music.

In virtually every choreographic creation by Garth Fagan there is an exceptional resonance, a haunting and touching vision of human desire and memory; a luminous encounter with the marvel as well as the terror of humankind. Implicit in Fagan's creative imagination is the capacity to evoke but never to state the profound themes of his dances. Their merit is found in their experience and not in their meaning. Such signature choreographic elements are everywhere visible in the Garth Fagan repertory. It would be difficult to name another choreographer of the last decade with the expressive originality and power of Garth Fagan. Here is a choreographer who touches upon the most sublime experience: that mythic place in human consciousness where thought and feeling merge.

11

My first encounter with the theatre work of Maurice Bejart took place in Brussels, about a year prior to his American debut. On that evening, the magnum opus was a massive work based on the poetry of Francesco Petrach, a dance-drama entitled *The Triumph of Time*. It is one of those full-evening productions for which Bejart is renowned — an extravaganza that fully filled the huge sports arena where it was staged. Loosely built on the epic series of poems by Petrach called *Trionfi* and employing a colorful succession of highly stylized and dramatic tableaux, the dance alludes to several famous Petrachian themes: the triumph of desire over humankind, the triumph of chastity over desire, of death over chastity, of fame over death, of time over fame, and, finally, the triumph of eternity over time.

When I first saw this massive theatre work, Americans had not yet seen any of Bejart's dances. We had heard about them, but few of us actually knew his choreography. For me, *The Triumph of Time* was an exceptional evening in the theatre; one for which I was completely unprepared, despite the fact that Bejart's reputation for opulence was much discussed and much debased in the American world of dance. The avalanche of startling theatrical gestures was quite beyond anything I had ever seen. I didn't know quite what to make of it. The utter giganticism of the presentation was something I had known only from the circus performances I had seen as a youth in America. How could a ballet company afford such grandeur? And what kind of an audience would want to see Bejart's Ballet of the Twentieth Century?

Jamake Highwater

The leonine head of Maurice Bejart.

Jamake Highwater

Two images from The Triumph of Time, choreographed by Maurice Bejart for the Ballet of the Twentieth Century.

Jamake Highwater

I was much aware that Bejart's skill as a magician of the theatre had won him both a substantial annual subsidy from the government of Belgium as well as a superstar reputation that attracted thousands upon thousands of people to his performances, but I was nonetheless thunderstruck by the fact that a mob of middle-class citizens applauded, stamped their feet, and cheered throughout the entire two-hour production. Clearly, this was a new notion of non-elitist "culture" which sophisticated Americans would find curious, at best.

When I returned to New York, I wrote a review of what I had seen for *Dance Magazine*, and in that review, I predicted, with considerable regret, that American dance critics would entirely miss the point of Maurice Bejart's theatre, and would probably use a good deal of print to express their contempt for his theatrical mannerisms. Unfortunately, I was right. Bejart's first American appearances were greeted with the kind of contempt that is usually reserved for mass murderers. How could it be otherwise?

It was the heyday of plotless, abstract dances by Merce Cunningham and George Balanchine. And so it was only natural that Bejart's work would be seen as grossly overstated, completely banal, utterly pretentious, and — worst of all — excessively popular! In those days in America we liked our art under glass.

Critics took Bejart's measure by comparing his grand theatrical gestures to the *zen* economy of Balanchine's masterful choreography. Where, the critics asked, was Bejart's choreography? Where was the *dance?* For the 1970s, these were understandable questions. We had yet to encounter performance art or the "operas" of Robert Wilson and Meredith Monk — creation in which artists took delight in mixing media and destroying the arbitrary boundaries between pop and art. Unable to see what was before them, because they could not see what they expected and what they wanted to see, most American critics decided that Bejart had replaced choreography with panache. As it turns out, I think they were wrong.

Maurice Bejart is anything but the charlatan of the theatre his critics often accuse him of being — a mere trickster who substitutes sleight of hand gimmicks for genuine talent. To the contrary, Bejart is a man of very considerable talent and a curious kind of genius. His theatre works are impelled by a poetic imagination that finds it necessary to re-invent dance in order to achieve his purposes. He envisions movement in architectural terms, not simply as it is made visible by the human body. For Bejart, the theatre is a living space in which every possible theatrical element is drafted into the service of his over-sized vision. But *vision* it is! Bejart is not a showman; he is more truly a postmodern shaman of the theatre, who uses excess and exaggeration to express the most fragile and subtle of human conditions. Bejart has no interest in striving for a microcosm which expresses a cosmic idea through a small and singular situation. He works from quite the opposite point of view, striving to create the semblance of the macrocosm as a theatrical experience. Bejart ritualizes human experience in gestures that are monstrously larger than life, very much like the theatrical forms familiar to us in the work of Richard Wagner. As such, Bejart is a rarity in the twentieth century: a theatre artist devoted to monumentality.

To claim that Maurice Bejart is excessive is to say exactly what he is. But, such an observation is not a denigration. For Bejart excess is a virtue.

12

The National Dance Company of Senegal is internationally renowned for its color, physicality, and ethnic authenticity. For more than a quarter century and during twenty global tours, the troupe of singers, dancers, and musicians has won accolades as one of Africa's most distinguished performing organization.

The company was founded, shortly after Senegal won its independence in 1959, by poet Maurice Senghor, nephew of then-President Leopold Senghor. Its mission was to stage tribal songs, dances, and ceremonies from the diverse peoples of this new nation — the Wolof, the Serer, the Dyola, the Peul, and the Tukulor — as a celebration of Senegal's many cultural heritages.

Today the company has become a source of popular entertainment, but two decades ago during its American debut, it caused a sensation; in many cities performances were canceled, while in others squads of police lined the aisles to prevent female dancers from appearing with bared breasts. Ironically, today the African dancers appear to be embarrassed by the nudity that was once so natural to them, while viewers of soap operas on American television are no strangers to bared bodies. This contradiction is both puzzling and highly provocative.

Today, at performances by the National Dance Company of Senegal, audiences respond with great exuberance. The music is loud. The dancing is frenetic. The costumes are bold and colorful. And the energy is volcanic. But, nonetheless, it is difficult to be convinced that the Senegalese company is much more than an ethnic replay of those dazzling "Flash Acts" that used to close vaudeville shows — a great deal of glitz and dazzle to make up for a lack of substance, which brings up a persistent problem in the presentation of ethnic culture to Western audiences.

Folklore cannot endure the theatrical exaggeration that producers use to turn ethnicity into commerce. This kind of commercialization is an almost unavoidable quandary for most ethnic companies, from the Mexican Folklorico to the Mazowsze Polish Dancers — groups that make valiant efforts to transport folk materials from their native worlds into the Western theatre.

There is something mutually exclusive about the intimate, culture-bound, participatory nature of ethnic rites and the quite contrary rituals of the commercial theatre. The very qualities of redundancy, naivete, and nonchalance that are so very attractive in ceremonies viewed in native settings become repetitious, pointless, boring, and highly self-conscious when viewed from a seat in the theatre.

Many critics and spectators respond to the Senegalese performers with great, unquestioning enthusiasm, despite the artificiality of the performance. Apparently there is among industrial populations a great longing for exotic experiences that touch upon those essential and primal motifs that were lost in the Western world long long ago. This hunger for an experience of "the heart of darkness" makes us quite willing to settle for "fakelore," a term Richard Dorson, the late Indiana University professor and author, devised to describe just the kind of art that is performed by the National Dance Company of Senegal.

What is most curious about the commercialization of ethnicity is the way it feeds upon itself, and turns back into its own culture and fundamentally changes it. We assume that the Senegal company is merely attempting to turn its 30-member ensemble into a commercially viable stage company. But something more insidious has taken place: By praising people for pleasing us, we have encouraged them to *become* us and to abandon themselves.

Today it is far easier to sit in an American theatre and scorn the tasteless elaborations of native costume that, for instance, the Senegalese dancers wear in their piece called *Mandinkole*, or to disapprove of the shrill amplification of native instruments like the kora and balafon than it is to recognize that such costumes and amplification have become intrinsic aspects of Senegalese culture. For twenty-five years our applause has indicated what we like, and, as a result, the people of Senegal have settled for a culture that pleases us. What they have pretended to be, for the sake of pleasing us, they have become.

This kind of ethnicide has taken place all over the world. And there is apparently no way to reverse its momentum. When I first visited Zaire and Mali,

The National Dance Company of Senegal performing from its diverse tribal heritage.

courtesy Jorgensen Auditorium, University of Connecticut, Storrs

the hospitable inhabitants were both fascinated and appalled by my Western dress, but only a decade later, when I returned, all the men were wearing jeans and were more than a bit embarrassed by the photographs I had previously taken of them in their native costumes.

In thinking about the Senegal company, I am struck by the possibility that black American choreographers like Pearl Primus and Garth Fagan have produced a more genuinely authentic and impassioned theatrical transformation of African culture than have the artists of today's Africa. Primus and Fagan understand the strength of their ethnic heritage at the same time that they evade the trivializing expectations of audiences. Their result is an *imaginary Africa* that is more real than the real Africa.

In contrast to the self-image of these American artists, the audience's view of Senegal seems to have become the Senegalese view. I came away from the performance of the National Dance Company of Senegal deeply distressed by a program of songs and dances that was sadly overproduced and drastically underrealized in terms of imagination and ideas.

The marvelously wide range of tribal movement had given way to hopelessly self-conscious pantomime in "choreographed ballets," as in *Mandinkole*, that were grim reminders of the results of the kind of Westernization that produces shiploads of ethnic ashtrays. At the same time that the themes and forms of the performance were compromised by commercialism, the incredible dance heritage of Africa was forsaken. There was an overwhelming dependence upon three or four persistently repeated movements of the legs. The narrative themes of the dances seem to have been drawn from romantic Hollywood melodramas. And with rare exception, the costumes were campy impersonations of Las Vegas exotica.

All that remained of an ancient and noble tradition was the exquisite refinement and complexity of the drumming, so brilliant and so highly evolved that it alone reminded us of the many worlds that have been lost to many of the descendents of the great and civilized tribes of Africa.

Vibrant drumming powers the National Dance Company of Senegal.

courtesy Jorgensen Auditorium, University of Connecticut, Storrs

It is the business of the future to be dangerous... the major advances in civilization are processes that all but wreck the societies in which they occur.

ALFRED NORTH WHITEHEAD,
Adventures in Ideas

CONCLUSION: THE FUTURE OF RITUAL

We stand on the horizon of a new century, when dance has achieved an unexpected reunion with the rites of our most ancient ancestry. It has emerged as something ever new and ever old.

Isadora Duncan brought into the twentieth century a romantic notion of the profound spirituality of the dances of antiquity. Vaslav Nijinky, Mary Wigman, and Martha Graham gave us a translucent vision of dance as an expression of ritualism and tribal mythology. These choreographic conceptions had a vast impact on all the modern art forms — music, painting, architecture, literature. Beginning with Fokine, this revolutionary "new dance" even infused the rather static mentality of the classic ballet with rare vitality and daring.

Then, quite suddenly, just when innovative dance began at long last to win a large, popular audience, a new rebellion began among the young. The much touted complexities and subtleties of modernism became unacceptable to a new generation of choreographers. Much as Graham had rejected the fairytale mentality of ballet in favor of a more human focus; just as Hawkins, Balanchine, and Cunningham had rejected the psychological realism of Graham in favor of non-programmatic and abstract idioms of dance; so a new 1980s generation of dancers rejected the reigning mentality of abstract modernism that had become the hallmark of art for sixty-five years, and they formulated a succession of highly individual and diversified choreographic attitudes that were given the name "postmodernism."

This apparent revolt in the choreographic arts was not so much a rebellion as a reassertion of the ideals of Isadora, Nijinsky, Graham, and all the other pioneers who believed that they had rediscovered the human soul in the rites of tribes and the mythos of antiquity. The postmodernists, like the modernists

ilson Pico, a choreographer from Ecuador whose work focuses on the
ual sagas of his country with the modernist influence of Cunningham.

before them, were attempting to bring dance back to its position of centrality as an expression of the human condition. They achieved their aims through a long series of collaborations with people in many different art forms, creating an idiom known as "performance art," a term that most of them have now come to disown.

The genre known in the 1980s as performance art was an innovative effort of choreographers as well as theatre directors and visual artists to realize an old idea. In the 1940s Antonin Artaud had called it the "Theatre of Cruelty," a revolutionary vision built on his conceptions and misconceptions of the Balinese ritual stage and his desire to destroy the materiality of language and social realism that he detested in the theatre. Artaud wanted to bring fresh vigor into the theatrical arts and to make actors and audiences into "victims burnt at the stake, signaling through the flames."

Earlier still, in the 1850s, Richard Wagner had called a similar revisionist notion of the theatre *gesammtkunstwerke* ("works of all-arts-in-one"). He melded all the arts into an organic and total theatre animated by *volkgeist*, the folk spirit implicit in a collective mythic mentality — a mentality which would become the focus of the work of Carl Jung.

Wagner and Artaud and many other artists have been deeply preoccupied with ritual, myth, dream states, the irrational, and the subconscious. This preoccupation has become a central, creative concern of our century. As Herbert L. Scheidau noted: "It may be that the most important development of twentieth-century consciousness has to do with atom bombs or moon walks, but with a new seriousness toward prehistory and mythology."

Mythologist Joseph Campbell dedicated his life to that new seriousness toward prehistory and mythology. "The seat of the soul," he wrote, "is where the inner and outer worlds meet."

> *The outer world changes with historic time. The inner world is constant. And so you have throughout the mythologies of people a constant. You always have the sense of recognizing something. And what you are recognizing is your own inward life. The problem of making this inner life meet the outer world of today is the function of the artist.*

Some of the most innovative artists of the eighties and nineties have managed to show us the fragile junction at which our inner and outer lives meet. To achieve this difficult task, they have redefined the limits of art and redrawn the arbitrary lines between various artistic disciplines. What has emerged is a theatre in which movement is the compelling and central force, the matrix that unifies the contributions of actors, dancers, painters, musicians, writers, and dramaturges. Just such an arrangement is found in a fine work by the Urban Bush Women called *Praise House* (1990).

Using dance, music, speech, song, and the visual arts to great theatrical effect, *Praise House* asks important questions about the spiritual experience of African-American artists whose work is devoted to the expression of a highly personal religious faith. Despite the fact that *Praise House* is ostensibly concerned with the life of the self-taught painter Minnie Evans, the impact of this exceptional

Cylla Von Tiedemann, courtesy Urban Bush Women

Urban Bush Women's production of *Praise House,* with company members Viola Sheely, Theresa Cousar (foreground), Grisha Coleman, Amy Pivar, Christine King and Marlies Yearby (left to right).

Cylla Von Tiedemann, courtesy Urban Bush Women

(Left to right) Laurie Carlos, Theresa Cousar and Viola Sheely in the "biographical" ritual *Praise House.*

theatre piece is not to be found in its ability to deal with the specific and the individual but, to the contrary, in its ritual approach to all people who strive to fathom that mythic place where, as Joseph Campbell observes, the inner and the outer worlds meet. *Praise House* wisely avoids realistic narration, and uses "biographical ritual" to turn a life story into a ceremony of gesture and metaphors that explores that illusive junction of the self and the world. *Praise House* portrays an ingenious cultural process, envisioned not as social history or as the biography of an individual but as the ritual of childhood in the life of a solitary black woman who saves herself and her sanity by becoming an artist. "Draw or die!" she admonishes herself as she struggles with the enormous pain of her alienation. "Draw or die!"

There have been a number of theatre works, like *Green Pastures*, that have attempted to use the music, dance, dialect, and folk mentality of African-Americans to transform the style and context of various biblical and classic epics. But they all approach the world of African-Americans rather frivolously and from the vantage of the dominant European cultures. *Praise House* takes quite the opposite approach, dealing with the black experience through the ritual forms that have emerged from black culture itself. The result, however, is not ethnic drama. To the contrary, because it speaks in the language of myth and ritual, *Praise House* is able to open the way from a specific view of the black experience to a vision of us all.

Another remarkable achievement in the new union of dance and the theatrical arts was the Hartford Stage production by Richard Foreman of playwright George Buchner's unfinished drama *Woyzeck*. From the peculiar 18th-century fragmentary drama, Foreman created a powerful ritual experience. To that end, he reinvented the theatre, designing a totally nonpictorial stage environment that functioned as a cosmic membrane in which the characters lived out their nightmarish lives. Foreman also brought a strong cinematic concept of time and space to his production, made possible by his marvelous sense of dance and movement. The body language of the performers — sliding, falling, rolling, and running — was completely outside naturalism while at the same time creating a delirious kind of exaggerated realism. The sound design, also by Foreman, was another integral aspect of this ritualized production, insinuating the horror that lurks behind Buchner's powerful dialogue, accenting the choreographed lovemaking and danced violence, and liberating the immense gentleness and longing of the tragic characters.

A theatre production of equal impact, which underscored the choreographic impulse that is the basis of so many major artistic achievements, was the Guthrie Theatre of Minneapolis offering of *Frankenstein: Playing With Fire* by playwright Barbara Field. Field has created a "response" to the ever-popular metaphor of Frankenstein and his monster, the Creature. As a play, *Frankenstein* owes a debt to Robert Montgomery's brilliant *Subject to Fits*, a neglected play of 1972 that was one of the first successful efforts to create a "response" to a work of literature (Dostoyevsky's novel *The Idiot*), rather than simply writing a faithful and literal dramatization of a familiar plot. This process of recreating a new work (a "response") from a classical source is a central focus of performance art. It is a process of ritualization that accents the half-conscious psychology of the artist's reservoir of responses to elements deeply entrenched in culture. It is a process of deconstruction and recreation, bringing about the ritualization of familiar aspects of culture in unfamiliar forms that resonate with things we somehow recognize. And, as Campbell noted, what we recognize in such experience is ourselves.

For all of the intriguing writing of playwright Field, *Frankenstein* could not readily be the creation of just one person. Like so much of what is called performance art, the production was probably the result of a long and complex creative association between artists of various disciplines, like those that evolve out of workshops, where experimentation, revision, and discovery transform works on paper into rituals of the theatre.

There are many other important examples of theatre works in which dance and movement have become the primary guiding and moving force. One thinks of the theatre of Robert Wilson, the innovative opera productions of Peter Sellars, and the ferociously emotional works of Pina Bausch. But probably the most luminous of this new breed of artist is Meredith Monk, who has created a series of extraordinary theatre and filmic works which celebrate the ritual union of music, movement, language, image, and the human spirit. Two theatre works, in particular, come to mind: the 1984 collaboration with Ping Chong called *The Games* and the 1991 opera called *Atlas*. In these works Meredith Monk has achieved a visionary translucence of extraordinary power and impact.

The setting for *The Games*, with company members.

Ruth Walz, courtesy The House Foundation

She allows us momentarily to encounter experiences entirely beyond our expectation. Meredith Monk is a magician of the unexpected. She understands the mythic and ritual process by which the shapeless takes shape and the ineffable finds a voice. She understands something about the ancient process of ritual that allows us to know the unknown through its countless mythic disguises. She understands that the body is the cosmos, for our mythologies about our place in the cosmos are inevitably transformed into anatomical metaphors. Rituals are mythologies transformed into bodily actions. Rituals are the embodiment of mythology, and myths are stories that recount the whole of a society's knowledge. Meredith Monk realizes that ritual is mind transformed into body. And this awareness makes it possible for her to create works of unmatched spirituality.

At the close of the twentieth century, we have come to realize that the body is Plato's cave on whose walls are cast the shadows we mistake for reality. We are Plato's creatures, forever bound in a cave so that even our heads cannot move. Behind us is a fire, and the shadows of a world we cannot see are cast upon the wall before us. We cannot escape our bonds. We can never look back at the *reality* that we imagine exists somewhere beyond our view. We must believe in the shadows, for we have no access to the reality they reflect. We can neither imagine nor speak of that reality because it is beyond our experience and outside our communicative capacities. The poet William Black believed that the body is Plato's cave and, therefore, he insisted rather sadly, "the body is the grave of the soul." But for dancers, like Meredith Monk, the body is indistinct from the soul.

What is it about a great dancer that transforms the body into spirit, that changes ordinary gesture into powerful ritual?

Dance changes biology into a metaphor of the spiritual body in much the way that poetry changes ordinary words into forms that allow meanings that words normally cannot convey. The most curious thing about any human gesture is its power of insinuation, born of the ability of the body to overcome its inherent materiality. That is precisely what Meredith Monk does for an audience when she turns the theatre into a reflection of our most inward selves. The new union of the arts in the theatre achieves the same things that poetry achieves. They transform the ordinary into the extraordinary. Through the sensual and metaphoric transformation of a reality composed of shadows they are able, at least momentarily, to allude to the fire.

Dance is that fire.

Company members in *The Games*, a collaboration of Ping Chong and Meredith Monk.

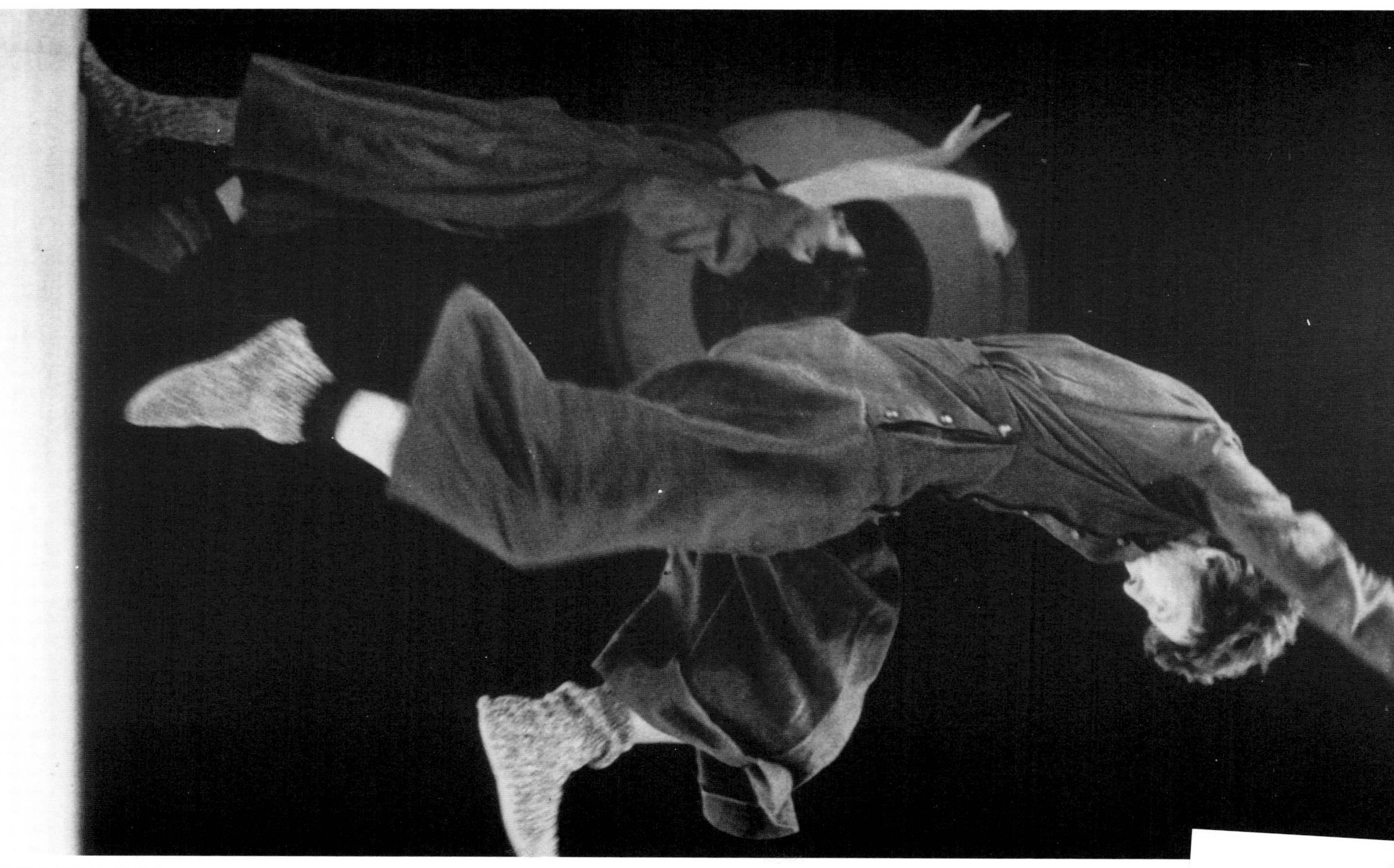

Ruth Walz, courtesy The House Foundation

,ography

Barnes, Harry, *An Intellectual and Cultural History of the Western World*, Reynal & Hitchcock, 1937. One of the classic overviews of the West; and an ideal source of an understanding of the way in which political, economic, philosophical, and artistic trends influence and grow out of each other.

Boas, Franziska, *The Function of Dance in Human Society*. Dance Horizons, 1944, 1972. An anthropological correlation between social structures and dance expressiveness.

H'Doubler, Margaret N., *Dance: A Creative Art Experience*, University of Wisconsin Press, 1940, 1957. A major discussion of the artistic and structural basis of dancing.

Dufrenne, Mikel, *The Phenomenology of Aesthetic Experience*, Northwestern University Press, 1973. The classic phenomenological treatment of art by the leading French existential philosopher of art.

Harrison, Jane Ellen, *Art and Ritual*, Henry Holt & Co., 1913. The viewpoint central to the Cambridge classical school of anthropology is applied by Harrison — a primer among works by Sir James Frazer (*The Golden Bough*), Gilbert Murray, and Joseph Campbell.

Haskell, Arnold L., *Ballet*, Penguin Books, Ltd., 1933. A basic approach to ballet from the viewpoint of a traditionalist.

Hess, Hans, *How Pictures Mean*, Pantheon Books, 1974. A radical and insightful interpretation of the aesthetic experience from the standpoint of the spectator.

Horst, Louis, *Pre-Classic Dance Forms*, Dance Observer, 1937. A pioneer discussion of the composition and social functions of the court dance forms which preceded ballet.

Kirstein, Lincoln, *Dance: A Short History of Theatrical Dancing*, Dance Horizons, 1969.

_____, *Three Pamphlets Collected: Blast at Ballet, Ballet Alphabet, What Ballet Is About*, Dance Horizons, 1969. A collection of essays which came to the aid of ballet during the era when modern dance and ballet were the basis of a conflict.

Langer, Susanne K., *Feeling and Form*, Charles Scribner's Sons, 1953.

_____, *Philosophy in a New Key*, Harvard University Press, 1942, 1951, 1957.

_____, *Problems in Art*, Charles Scribner's Sons, 1957. Three books which perpetuate a metaphoric view of language and a nonsyntactical view of art — depicting art as a symbolic process.

Lloyd, Margaret, *The Borzoi Book of Modern Dance*, Alfred A. Knopf, 1949. The first major collection of profiles and appraisals of the founders and first several generations of modern dancers.

Martin, John, *America Dancing*, Dance Horizons, 1968. The first major proponent of modern dance offers a rationale for expressionism in dance.

Read, Sir Herbert, *Art and Society*, Schocken Books, 1966. A study of the relationships of art and society.

_____, *The Philosophy of Modern Art*, Horizon Press, 1953. An important early treatise on the sensibility of the modern persuasion in art generally, and in the graphic arts particularly.

Sorell, Walter (ed.), *The Dance Has Many Faces*, Columbia University Press, 1966. Several views of dancing by major artists and critics.

Sachs, Curt, *World History of the Dance*, W. W. Norton & Co., 1937. The pioneer history of "popular" dance forms from antiquity to the emergence of Isadora Duncan.

Index

Note: italic page numbers refer to captions and photographs.